BNP

OTHER EDITIONS IN THIS SERIES

George Garrett, guest editor, *Best New Poets 2005*

Eric Pankey, guest editor, *Best New Poets 2006*

Natasha Tretheway, guest editor, *Best New Poets 2007*

Mark Strand, guest editor, *Best New Poets 2008*

Kim Addonizio, guest editor, *Best New Poets 2009*

Claudia Emerson, guest editor, *Best New Poets 2010*

D.A. Powell, guest editor, *Best New Poets 2011*

Matthew Dickman, guest editor, *Best New Poets 2012*

Brenda Shaughnessy, guest editor, *Best New Poets 2013*

Dorianne Laux, guest editor, *Best New Poets 2014*

Tracy K. Smith, guest editor, *Best New Poets 2015*

Mary Szybist, guest editor, *Best New Poets 2016*

Natalie Diaz, guest editor, *Best New Poets 2017*

Kyle Dargan, guest editor, *Best New Poets 2018*

Cate Marvin, guest editor, *Best New Poets 2019*

Brian Teare, guest editor, *Best New Poets 2020*

BEST NEW POETS

2021

50 Poems from Emerging Writers

Guest Editor Kaveh Akbar

Series Editor Jeb Livingood

This book is published in cooperation with *Meridian* (readmeridian.org) and the University of Virginia Press (upress.virginia.edu).

For additional information, visit us at
bestnewpoets.org
twitter.com/BestNewPoets
facebook.com/BestNewPoets

Cover design by 4 Eyes Design, 4eyesdesign.com

Text set in Adobe Garamond Pro and Gill Sans

Printed by Bailey Printing, Charlottesville, Virginia

ISBN: 978-0-9975623-5-4
ISSN: 1554-7019

Contents

About Best New Poets ix

Nancy Miller Gomez, Siren Song 1
Tarik Dobbs, Dragphrasis: Alexis Mateo Calls Home the Troops with a Death Drop 2
Katherine Hur, Nineteen Sixty-Three: Year of the Rabbit 3
Lauren Licona, the first creation story i ever heard 4
Caitlin Cowan, Miscarry 6
Yvette R. Murray, Strangeness³ 7
Karisma Price, My Phone Autocorrects "Nigga" to "Night" 8
Michael VanCalbergh, A Creation Myth 10
Zebulon Huset, [Start at the Beginning] 16
Caitlin Roach, Derivations 17
Kristina Martino, All I Can Have Are Field Recordings of the Field 22
Jay Yencich, Demonym 24
Samyak Shertok, No Rhododendron 25
Sharon Lin, An Offering at the Altar 30
Alicia Rebecca Myers, Winter Solstice 32
Aaron Magloire, In Which I Travel to Alternate Dimensions in Search of Healing After Another Black Man is Shot by Police 33
Boston Gordon, Clinical Assessment of Gender Identity 38

Natalie Tombasco, Nomenclature 40
Bryce Berkowitz, Microwaving Sub Sandwiches in the Trailer 42
Nicole Caruso Garcia, Is This Your Cow? 43
Su Cho, How to Say Water 46
April Freely, Every Verb is a Lesson in Longing or Dread 47
Nathan Lipps, How to Believe 48
Sadia Hassan, A List of Places I Am [ ] 49
Henry Goldkamp, The Our Daddy 52
Margaret Ray, First, and Then, and Then 54
Tyler Starks, Walk It Off Octopus 56
Marissa Davis, Marketplace 57
Jennifer Sutherland, Positioning 60
Katelyn Botsford Tucker, House for Sale 61
Mandy Gutmann-Gonzalez, Sarah Good's Confession 62
Erin L. McCoy, How a Lake Flash-Froze a Herd of Horses 64
Jane Huffman, Six Revisions 65
Patrick James Errington, Not an Elegy 68
Grace Wang, Zodiac Year of the Lamb 70
Remi Recchia, Dead Name 72
David Joez Villaverde, Granizo, or Apologia Pro Lustro 75
Kyle Carrero Lopez, After Abolition 80
Jessica Lynn Suchon, Adultery 81
Micah Ruelle, The Last Birthday Gift 82

JinJin Xu, To Red Dust (II) 83
Adam J. Gellings, Second Person 90
Mary Ardery, Fourth-Grade Soundtrack 92
Chris Crowder, On the Street Marked “Dead End” 94
huiying b. chan, how we survived: 爺爺’s pantoum (i) 96
Augusta Funk, Poem in My Mother’s Voice 99
Gavin Yuan Gao, Myth, or Luck as a Swan Boat 100
Hannah Perrin King, Transcript of My Mother’s Sleeptalk: Chincoteague 102
Hannah Matheson, Daniel Johnston 104
Rebecca Zweig, This Poem Has a One-Night Stand 106

Acknowledgments 109
Contributors’ Notes 113
Participating Magazines 125
Participating Programs 133

About Best New Poets

Welcome to *Best New Poets 2021*, our seventeenth annual anthology of fifty poems from emerging writers. At *Best New Poets* we define "emerging writer" narrowly: our anthology only features poets who have not published a book-length collection of their own poetry. Our goal is to provide special encouragement and recognition to poets just starting in their careers, the many writing programs they attend, and the magazines that publish their work.

From February to May of 2021, *Best New Poets* accepted nominations from writing programs and magazines in the United States and Canada. Each program and magazine could nominate two writers, and those poets could send a free submission to the anthology. For a small entry fee, writers could also submit poems as part of our open competition. Eligible poems were either published after January 1, 2020, or unpublished. Which means you are not only reading new poets in this book, but also some of their most recent work.

In all, we received just under 2,000 submissions for a total of nearly 3,700 poems. A pool of readers and the series editor ranked these submissions, sending a few hundred selections to this year's guest editor, Kaveh Akbar, who chose the final fifty poems that appear here.

Nancy Miller Gomez

Siren Song

A songbird mimicking the sounds of emergency sirens has been caught on video.
—CNN

A starling has taught himself to sing
like an ambulance. Now the air is filled

with emergencies. *Whee-o, whee-o,* high and low,
a fire truck rides out of a mockingbird's mouth.

Grackles impersonate police cars. They dive-bomb
the precinct parking lot, bashing their beaks

into the rearview mirrors of their rivals.
The magpie knows a lovely air raid. Now

she trills like a helicopter, next a chain saw,
then an AK-47. The quail stop, drop

and cower. *Take-CO-ver* they cantillate.
Whee-o, whee-o, high and low. Juncos,

pass to vireos. Catbirds steal the flow.
The chickadees have gone on lockdown.

They bore like bullets through the bleeding bark
of the cedars. Crows reload from rooftops.

Tarik Dobbs

Dragphrasis: Alexis Mateo Calls Home the Troops with a Death Drop

BAM BAM BAM BAM BAM BAM
BAM BAM BAM BAM BAM
BAM BAM BAM BAM BAM BAM
BAM BAM BAM BAM BAM
BAM BAM BAM BAM BAM BAM
BAM BAM BAM BAM BAM
BAM BAM BAM BAM BAM BAM
BAM BAM BAM BAM BAM
BAM BAM BAM BAM BAM BAM

Even if I was born on the moon…

I coat my eyelids in a toothpaste full of stars

…I would still be an American

I excavate the basement dress-up chest

[She twirls] in my sister's ball gown & an aunt's cancer wig, I'm Hannah Montana

Yes, baby before RuPaul's laugh, before Mosul was collapsing, before me as witness

I rise in that mirror so proud, a haram-bomb girl, my mom says, I made my own doll

Katherine Hur

Nineteen Sixty-Three: Year of the Rabbit

In Korean folklore   after a beggar asks for food   a rabbit throws itself into a cooking fire
having nothing to offer but its own body   except turns out this beggar is actually
the Emperor of the Heavens in disguise!   and he appoints Rabbit as guardian of the moon
a grand reward   only   surprise   there isn't any food on the moon   so now
Rabbit has to spend an eternity alone at a mortar   pounding rice cakes on the moon to eat
and I always thought that was the saddest part of the story   but my mother only ever talked
about the sacrifice   and though she didn't throw herself into a fire   she did hang herself
from a black walnut tree   which my father once said is good for woodwork   straight-grained
richly colored   and it's hardwood   so it took him hours to fell with an ax
and he refused to carve it into two-by-fours for a casket   instead he left the tree in the yard
like another dead thing   and I knew it was a walnut tree because years ago   at summer camp
I learned about nature and survival   how to survive in the wilderness   and how to identify
things that might kill you   which could be anything   a fire   a tree   your family.

Rabbit, lucky Rabbit, Rabbit in the moon.
The prize for your sacrifice is exile,
the price for your burning is the moon,
from which we have hung your body.

—Nominated by *The Southern Review*

Lauren Licona

the first creation story i ever heard

goes like this: in the beginning, there was no light.
everything that existed was a deep sleep.
a mother stirs in the long night she rears, and names it absence.
from absence, she makes two sons, one son makes man, another
makes war. man makes a sword, makes la ballista, makes gunpowder,
and kills the sons, kills the mother. it is from their blood you are given
genesis, mission, decimation, and the colonial church. after a few hundred years
you are given an american flag, no generators, a tin roof, and paper towels for a flood.

*

the word hurricane is taíno—from hurakán, phonetic descendent of juracán:
god of the storm, second self-willed son, who brought his chaos to the west.
summers of rage, i remember. calabash tree through kitchen window, no running water.
a drowned shore, dead fish fetid and bleaching under an exiled sun. remember, how luis
died stepping on a live wire? i read somewhere that *electricity is just lightning pretending*
to be permanent, maybe it is the same for the storm. maybe it is the same for the flood.
remember, remember, the cries and himnos in the dark of those forty nights?

*

"*you are native before you are american,*" is one of the few things i can recall my father telling me.
i thought this meant being tapped into a primordial grief. my displaced rage, my native guard.
inside me, an acreage and an armada of ships, of men waged from absence. what i wage
is far worse. after all, it was i who inherited the sleeplessness, the torrent, the flag, the gun

tossed into the sea. it was i who fashioned this great loneliness, who threw my arms around
each wandering son i loved and whispered "ven a casa." come home to a place that cannot
exist again. cariño, natiao, tell me where will you run from the powers that come
to thrash and skin and bleed you?

*

i open for a lover against the seawall of a river named mantazas. spanish for massacre.
a few close centuries ago, hundreds of shipwrecked men lined themselves along this shore
and presented their necks. we grow along these estuaries of blood.
i salvage what i can at the edge of a mouth, at the ellipse
of a body, water racking the skin of my many griefs. i became what birthed me,
with a storm in the passage of my throat.

the story will end how it begins: a long night, a woman labored
with the first emptiness. she writhes, opening her mouth, expelling light.

Caitlin Cowan

Miscarry

The president's spiritual advisor called for the fruits
of *satanic wombs* to *miscarry* two days before I discovered
the blueberry growing in me, four days before the mothwing
of its heart stopped winking in double time. Every time
I write *mothwing,* someone whispers *mothering,* turns me
into something I am not. The stained towel strewn
on the highway is not a crane from the nearby marsh. Notice
I avoided the word *stork:* storks have no syrinx, which is
one way to say they have no voice. Cranes are very vocal,
like the pair I watched on TV to numb out those first weeks.
Two brothers. Everything is babies. Grief is a hollow
whose depth never changes, a perfect post hole for a fence
love wants to build but can't. How's this for satanic: I kept the jar
of good blood like a beating heart, let it loom like red meat
in the fridge. It was cold. I am cold. Damn the heart-shaped
teratoma they lift from a friend's empty womb. Damn
the president. Full of teeth and hair, hers was no child
but could have been for the awe it seeded in her. It might be a letter
that never reached its destination, quite simply not carried, slipped
from the mailbag like a leaf, grown quiet as a moth's wing
still beneath its own dust. When our letters are delivered,
in this world or another, I imagine the someone who reads them.

Yvette R. Murray

Strangeness^3

Dark, magnolia scented air
Witness to burning flesh
punctuated by a rope creak
is the worst way to die
Don't blame the South
It's cotton's fault
Rice; indigo are guilty too
The beauties of dark skin
It's too heavy to bear
So you weighed down poplars.
with my many lives
took souvenirs to lovely homes.
Rope creak echoes
pound deep, deep, forevermore

Dark, sunlight of city streets
is a knee on a neck
or a runner not running
No worse way to live.
Blame the South.
No, it's greed's fault.
Sparkling brown eyes
incense old war wounds
and too many ghosts to fear.
A hunt begins
that never stopped.
Replay video; go viral
hold services; make speeches
and change nothing

Dark, skin infuriating
Crime of Being
A black thing dying
You can't live anymore!
Don't blame me.
Blame your Black self.
and your Black brilliance
What's yours is not mine
I rip more and I take.
In fear I stomp
With ancestors' blood running
An inherited agony
They did what I do
pound deep, deep, forevermore

Karisma Price

My Phone Autocorrects "Nigga" to "Night"

My nights
play cousin to
their mother's favorite
kettles. My nights won't consume
their reflections so they pour milk
in their coffee. My nights never rest
so they sing their shadows to sleep. Sometimes
they don't remember any words. My nights have frogs
stuck in their throats, no light soul, every bit of pain, my nights
all Louis Armstrong minus a trumpet, and my nights play chicken
with the train. My nights both shoe and polish. Both Sambo and Bruce
Leroy. We all little pretty medallions on our grandmothers' nightstands. My nights
are mistaken for other nights that bear no resemblance. I saw the sinew of the oldest night
in the neighborhood on the floor, his saint pendant missing. All the small, down feathered nights
scatter from the groan of pig sirens. My nights don't know their history. My nights are pecans without
the trees that grow them. My nights instruct all the people in their head to weep. My nights hate the firefly
cutting their darkness. *My night, did you see them? They just walked right passed us and didn't even speak.* My nights are ordinary,
wear ruffled socks, have the best belts. My nights don't always go to church but my nights are lambs worthy
of the morning. My nights are revised constitutions, crypt keepers, my nights are a congregation
of alligators on a rumpus bayou. My nights hiss into themselves. No one hears. Their blood
rolls its eyes. My nights chew gum and sunflower seeds. My nights eat pork. My nights
get the itis and slur their speech. My nights protest protests. The government
watches. My nights live in Brazil Botswana the Congo Cuba the D.R. France
Grenada Greece Honduras Ireland Liberia Lithuania Nigeria Venezuela
Zimbabwe. My nights live in America to remind you of me. Some

people think my nights are better with their eyes closed but
my nights have beautiful corneas. My nights wash clothes
that don't belong to them and won't look their bosses
in the eye. My nights know necessity. My nights
oblige. When my nights die, I wash them on
my kitchen table. After my nights are
washed, I throw away the table.
My nights have names. My
nights smell of sage.
My nights smell
of the muddy
rivers they
will never
swim in
again.

—Nominated by *Poetry*

Michael VanCalbergh

A Creation Myth

In the beginning, there's a child.
He kills his own cat, eats its liver.

His reward is a boat trip to a Michigan bar.
He's handed a towel. Eventually, he steals the keys.

He continues to devour livers.
He has a son who has a son who has a son

who doesn't. As he dies he misremembers
the cat's name, calls it a horseman.

*

In the beginning, there's an egg.
It's shaped like my family. It's passed
from one set of hands to another

to mine. Then, it cracks.
When I look, there is so much screaming
I lose my sense of smell.

This is where dissociation comes from.

*

In the beginning, my great-grandfather built a bridge.
His bones made the framework, his back the deck, his arms stretched
until his fingers became the abutment. My grandfather gave his eyes
to watch for intruders. My father stayed behind to hold his father
upright. It was noble. I was happy to change the lightbulbs
that eventually went out. Maybe one day, I thought,
I could give myself, too, to this.

*

In the beginning all things existed simultaneously,
    were metaphors,
obfuscated each other. It wasn't chaos.

It was ordered. Peripheral, sure, but ordered.
    Even with so much order,
eventually, truth will strip itself away and escape.

*

In the beginning
        of this poem,
                I couldn't say
                        I'm a myth. Each line,

neatly shrouded,
        etched in my skin.
                  A story
                        with no context.

*

In the beginning, why are there men?
Where are my mother's grandparents? Why
do I remember so little
about them? How could I forget
their stories? Why don't I ask?
Am I not their body too? Good
and bad, don't I breathe with them?

*

In the beginning   my parents   lied
to each other.   They told
each other that   they lied.   Neither
believed the other was capable   of such honesty.

*

In the beginning, I dug
underneath the Christmas tree. The stand
seemed so sturdy but as I went deeper
it crumbled. Pieces fell, revealed
I was in a cloud; the ocean below.
The heat from the light warmed my face.
I wanted more. I dove and

my father caught me,
dangling a cigarette
between his lips.

My mother took it
from his mouth,
breathed deep, said,
"Come here, sweetie."

*

In the beginning, my father dove to the bottom of our local pool. He reemerged with a small amount of shame.

I took it, spread it across as much empty space as I could. My mother saw me struggling

to work the shame into everything. She took what remained and spread it

further than I could see. To this day, I stumble upon palaces she built complete with mazes and motes.

They are so beautiful, I weep.

*

In the beginning it wasn't all bad.
There was tender laughter.
Clothes were worn till they tore
and new ones came after.
And we still ate.
We still created.
We lived.

*

In the beginning we are white.

Sometimes immigrants
but always white. So white
that my grandmother doesn't remember
which parents' parent or their parent came here when.
She says we have British and Russian ancestry.
These are the whitest places she knows.

This too makes me.

*

In the beginning I wasn't sorry.
I am now. Sorry for the lateness, for

the inadequacy of apology.
Sorry, in advance, to my mother who

will hear this poem, ask me what it means.
I won't know what to say. She'll be angry.

That's not my intent. Still, I continue
though inescapably this will be.

*

In the beginning I wanted forgiveness I haven't yet earned.
I won't explain everything. I keep dark the places
I'm not yet ready to go. Forgive me grandpa,

for I did tell some truths. Yes, you stole fire
from your father-in-law and gifted it to your children.
You also sold the original ember

you promised your prodigal son, leaving him.
He still waits for you.

*

In the beginning, I look down at the worlds I leave behind.
They are filled with pain
                                        and popcorn
                                                                    and passion
                                                                                        and places
                                                                                                        and people.
            More confluence of events than seems plausible.
            A braid of wire knotted around itself.
            The chromosome I can only see as I separate the starts from now.
            Harsh sounds.
            Hands that touched mine, gave me the strength to climb to a place where I'm
                        disappointed with who I am.
            How vain I was to think otherwise.
            I look forward to beginning.

Zebulon Huset

[START AT THE BEGINNING]

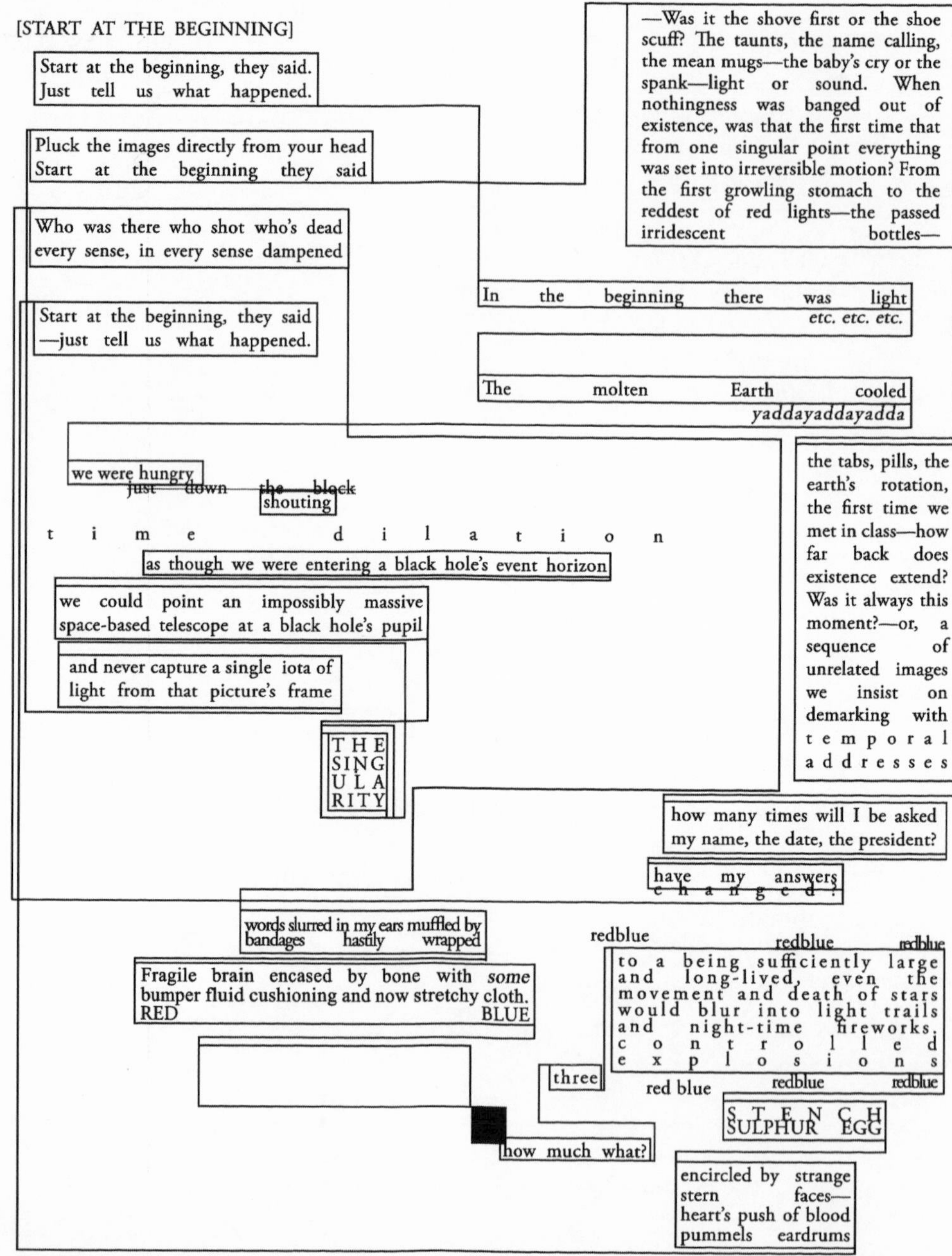

Caitlin Roach

Derivations

I hoped to call it *blue-black* but he did. Instead,
vampire squid and its glowing of itself

at its pockets to trick what's after it, twin eyes
dilating on a webbed-skin cloak it slips inside-

out to bare photophores, not eyes, and turns
them on like a switch, modulating their blue light

to confuse its hunter's understanding of space
between them. It's perception of separation

that matters in deep-sea purlieu. All that
glowing happens in blooms from scales

so small as to be near invisible, certainly
to the unescorted eye, hubcap-shaped on the single-

celled phytoplankton swelling like smoke
plumes in water. I said instead mountains,

whole ranges under the sea like an extra set
of teeth. Too, the sunflower sea star who thinks

at its mouth, *extruding its stomach* from it as if
from nowhere, the flat-limbed flesh lapping

up hapless dollars, *liquefying their soft parts*
until nothing is left except their white skeletons

which slink out from under the star's thick lip
when it's done with it until the current turns

what's left of them all belly-up, the blanched
wafers shuffling like chips underwater. Imagine

beginning life with five arms and dying
with twenty-one more. The octopus

and its three hearts race across the seafloor,
blue blood running cold through its nine brains.

We need consider what makes something move
ontogenetically, conceding its whole develop-

mental history, conditions which force it
to flee. There's no mimicry like that

of the octopus passing for others in its order.
We can learn assimilation tact from those

great benthic actors who carry their intelligence
in their arms, their becoming other to better

blend in out of necessity, not wish. Every body
I've ever known yearns for itself. That

the vampire squid has remained practically
unchanged for two hundred million years

before it split into ten-limbed squid and eight-limbed
octopuses must be some kind of miracle.

It's been named a living fossil, *the only known*
surviving member of its order. He's adapted so well

to the culture they'll say of my son when he speaks
unaccented English. He dangled at the end

of our cord like a fat fish, twitching and ready
to eat. *Phyto* roots in the Greek *phuein* meaning *come*

into being. My husband says a name is a site
to investigate power so we'll call our daughter *X*

because it's strong, pushing everything away from it,
rigorously resisting all attempts to restrain it. The sunchoke

takes no root in Jerusalem nor artichokes but is
a species of sunflower, distant relative of the daisy.

It's said Puritans named it after the New Jerusalem
they called the New World, the New World

having come into being for millennia. Recite me
the difference between *quiet* and *quell, arrive* and

colonize, exit and *escape* and I'll relay it to this fetus
that's newly gained hearing inside me. Last week

I heard a woman say she didn't know how much
more she could take. She saw him jump

from his balcony, she saw him fall she echoed
in the next breath and took me in

that distance built by revision of *jump*
to *fall.* I heard that when you drop out

it will sound like a fig splitting open.
She was blue-black edited to *she was born so blue*

having held her breath so long they said instead
of *nuchal asphyxiation.* I heard a species of spider

can weave a diving bell underwater, a silk
bubble that acts as a gill, extracting oxygen

from everything around it. It carries air
from the surface on its belly, covered

in hydrophobic hairs, and pumps its dome
full of it. Net diffusion of it in, net diffusion

of use returned out, little conductors
of breath to the underworld. Strange,

isn't it, a fear of water for a thing that lives
exclusively among it. *Argyroneta* stems from *argyros*

meaning *silver,* and *neta*, a vogue word, derived
from *neo,* meaning *spin,* and thus we arrive at *silver*

spinner, or *spinner of silver,* the tinge of import
decided by the mouth it spins in. At any rate,

they trap small fish in those bells.
When they sense something hit it *they dash*

out to paralyze it before pulling it into
the aquatic blister clung to the plant

they've held hostage. I heard once
a spider's silk is stronger than steel,

that a pencil-thick thread of it would halt
a Boeing 747 mid-flight.

Quotation sources, in order of appearance: 1. "Ocean Deep," PBS *Planet Earth*. 2. "Mysteries of the Deep," Monterey Bay Aquarium Research Institute. 3. "Vampire Squid," *Wikipedia*. 4. Seltzer, Leon, "What's So Fascinating About the Letter X?" PsychologyToday.com, March 3, 2016. 5) Bhanoo, Sindya N., "The Diving Bell and the Underwater Spider," *New York Times,* June 13, 2011.

Kristina Martino

All I Can Have Are Field Recordings of the Field

I can never have the field. I can never halve the field,
make a helix of my hands and hold the halves

like pictures of the field—or fields—and affix one feeling
to the fields—or the infinite field—*and stay that way.*

I can walk down to the bog, the field under-foliate-feet,
in a bloodflow motion towards the beating

of the bullfrogs' black-lacteous tactile pool
and listen to the unilluminable below-surface stirring,

gravid ruckus of drooling purr and primordial bluebrown blur.
I can aggravate the grating godhood and glisten

of preening slime—its opaque, plumbeous, tympanic
slurps—an inside-outside alertness *bur-bur-bur-bur-*

burrowing, harping with pings and plops (lurches),
and make the mossy froth go berserk with silence,

then foofaraw when the bog in the field senses I am
nothing to fear. I can hear amphibious *amour fou* pulsing

under a blue-green gasoline film, spongiform but formless,
boiling with blotched air-bubble let-go, life fumping

the surface in slicks of upward rain and glossopalatine pops
and liquid crop circles. I can stop here and listen,

in time with the bobolink and make my bel memento,
my untremendous tremolo and rinky-dink dictation.

In the fable, the animal smells fear and so does the fool.
I think to myself—in my skull's skeletal bell-shape—

I am both. I am both. I am both, and I can hold it together.

Jay Yencich

Demonym

If a true name grants power then it follows a false one
might perform alternate functions. Far easier if the world had wanted
names: Point and declare, this
"a zirconium," or that, "a figure
for light's first jagged ascent out of what we believe
to be a mouth, or the edge of a blade
or maybe both." That is not to say we have taken
to heart all the proper terms, only that we sometimes have loved
a sound heard once, thought it becoming of us,
and sowed our crop of nightshade, intent
on its blooms, the intricacy of its veins, not realizing
we were calling out to each other, "enemy, my enemy..."

Samyak Shertok

No Rhododendron

> *Between 1996 and 2006, an internal conflict between the Government of Nepal and the Communist Party of Nepal (Maoist) left at least thirteen thousand people dead and thirteen hundred missing.*
>
> —United Nations Office of the High Commissioner for Human Rights

They came unarmed. They came
half-masked. They came
before the crow. They came
with the moon. They came
moonless. They came
out of rain. They came
as their enemy. They came
smiling.

/

They slaughtered the goats. In burlap sacks, they gathered the pressure cookers, batteries, rusted rifles, madals, flashlights, transistor radios. For *your freedom.* They burned the books. They plucked the prayer bells from the lintels. They disappeared into the needlewoods.

/

They said People. They said Equality. They said One house, one soldier.

/

They parceled up his fingers in the paper containing his feature article and left it on the editor's desk.

/

They took my son from school while I was harvesting sugarcane. Three days later, we found his clothes flung up in a sacred fig tree. His naked body buried to the neck under the bridge. Green leaves wreathed his head. One eye was open.

/

You sheltered the enemy of the state.
        You mean your enemy we didn't say.
You fed terrorists.
        Like yourselves we didn't say.
You're the enemy of the state.
        They forced themselves into the house.
So they came.

/

They drank the milk tea I had made for my husband. He never returned. They tied my father's hands with his suruwal. He never returned. My son was studying for his district-level finals. He never returned. *Not even an eyelash will be missing.* My daughter never returned.

/

We couldn't tell whether they were Those-Who-Make-You-Disappear
or Those-Who-Walk-at-Night.

/

The vermillion blackened on my hair parting is a metaphor
for the vermillion blackened on my hair parting.

/

They said No red scarves. They said No pointing at the stars. They said
No rhododendron.

/

They made him whet the khukuri on a rock. They tied him to the hog plum
tree with his scarf in the middle of the playground. They handed the khukuri
to a former student. The commander barked. He stood cane-still. The commander
barked. He stood cane-still. The commander barked. He swung. The tree fell.
Thick red veined the bark. *If anyone touches the body…*

/

We couldn't tell whether we were dreaming.

/

They made my daughter say what they wanted to hear with a water heater live wire. They recorded her voice with her phone. They drank our homemade rum. Then they took turns.

/

Anyone seen outside after dusk will be shot on sight.

/

They made him dig the hole. They scooped his kneecaps with a broken Coca-Cola bottle and buried him.

/

The sugar in the tea you're drinking now came from the same field.

/

Crows tore the sky above.
No one went near the plum trunk.
A stray bitch kept guard.

/

You who plucked the full moon from my forehead
show me his bones.

/

They washed their hands in the Mikli-Phoom.
They drank the Mikli-Phoom from their clean cupped hands.

/

I returned to my bonded labor. I set the field on fire. Through the night I cut
the burning canes.

Sharon Lin

An Offering at the Altar

The monks from temple
drowned me in my infancy
with makko and frankincense

dusted my navel for the sins
of my past life—left it red and heavy
with oil and milk. It was scalded

as Buddha's feet were on the Phalgu River
where he trailed the banks to avoid
fire ants. Father gripping the prayer

wheel with my small hands
as he showed me how a life spins
itself into misfortune. In the morning

rubbing my toes with sand-
paper, shaving my scalp
until all I can count are the bones

of my skull. He tells me I trembled
as a crane before water, that
rebirth is a flight

in time, that all bones are
made from other bones. I was
a crane in my past life

born with arms above my head
as if in flight. Skin as light
as a sun the monks had to shadow

from to snip the cord. Feathers
when I fell to the earth
as my mother had fallen to the

sky. How she tore me out of
reach, anchored herself
to the stars. When Father held

prayer beads to his heart
whispering how one can never lose
that which is never yours. I

ask myself whether to trade a life
or to ascend. I would trade
this earth just to know.

Alicia Rebecca Myers

Winter Solstice

The Northern Hemisphere leans as far away from the sun as possible. A week ago, a construction worker fell five stories and survived by landing in a dumpster. I watched it happen from our window, propped up in bed purchasing The Clapper, only I mistook the ragged movement of rooftop specks for comradery. Our son wants the promise of no more fumbling through darkness. When we called the Santa hotline, he clapped twice to emphasize his wish. One Clapper reviewer notes that people with memory loss might forget how to press a button but never how to put their hands together. In the account of how the man fell, witnesses report he had unclipped from his gear to go home for the night. I read this as *unclapped.* I used to think the floors of a building were called stories, as in narrative. Story fifteen: I can now tie my hair under my chin! Story ninety-seven: I pull socks from the dirty hallway pile, too defeated to do laundry! This morning, in remote learning, I overhear the moon has low gravity. I want to ask if a mother can stumble off its crust. I got my tracker number for The Clapper and thought: "How are you so unwilling to touch a switch when you hang on me all the time?" and also: "Please stay little." Yesterday, I found a lotto card in the snow that wasn't a winner. It contained the words *same* and *wait* but also *rowboat.* All of the children are asked to unmute and howl at the screen, and after they're done, I put my hands together.

Aaron Magloire

In Which I Travel to Alternate Dimensions in Search of Healing After Another Black Man is Shot by Police

In one dimension, I mail a dead bird
to every white person who reposts the video

In another I cry
for the first time in two summers

It is always summer

In one I eat fruits, gorge myself,
vomit, and with the vomit spell names

Redoshi
Tamir
Aunt Sarah
Boy
Allthesame
To Be Sold & Let
Louis

In one I meet every slave
that ever jumped ship.
They have turned into Tahitian oyster pearls

In the next I sell the pearls to a white man for one month's rent

In each it is already summer,
unyieldingly hot

In one it's dry heat, a high
of 105 degrees
like in Sedona, the July
Philando and Alton died. I pretend
I'm part of the Red Rocks.
They let me sleep there a while

I dream
like Martin, like mountaintop
but don't wake up dancing

In one I'm watching a classic Western
but every cowboy is black

In one I'm watching a classic Western
but every cowboy is Black, capital B

Every black is capital

Speaking of dreams,
when I was a child
from time to time
I dreamt
I was falling

in blackness
always rolling forward
building momentum, but
somehow never managing
to go anywhere.

At least there
I am a child.
In some I'm not
or think I might be or
want to be but
can't tell for sure

In one I yanvalou dance at a cop's funeral

In one the funeral's mine

In one I cut the hair I've been growing all summer,
sever the chances
I'll be seen as a threat

In one I heal
from the men
but not the women, the children

The babies
brownskinned
buried

A white news anchor called Michael Brown a man the other day
it'd been six years since he died but he was
younger than me I still think of myself as a kid
ain't I a kid, still?

My father always talks about how I'm his only son
and I can't tell if it's a thing of pride or a thing of fear

There's always fear, stuck
unmoving as a body on the asphalt.
A kid on the asphalt
A man on the asphalt

It's still summer

In one I ask God "When?" and hear nothing
but smell smoke

In another He passes the phone to Noah, who says
Now

I think of that line from *Beloved*:
All of it is now it is always now
though there's something, especially,
about August

The birds come back stamped
Return to Sender.

In more than one there is no God

In every dimension I'm so angry I shake.
In every dimension I'm a flesh-
heavy bough I shake
the leaves from me I shake
the bodies from me I shake

the sweat from me
the summer from me
the blood from me
the time from me

I'm bare now, only the whisper
of something. A place
I've been before.
A dream I dreamt
a few times
as a child

Boston Gordon

Clinical Assessment of Gender Identity

What does the smell of lavender mean to you?
Sage? Mint? Rotten pine wood?
When you wear lipstick do you see yourself
as male or female? What is appropriate
length to keep one's armpit hair?
When a sudden noise startles you in the night
do you pretend to be brave?
Which celebrities do you want to be?
Which celebrities do you want to fuck?
If you were tasked to lift a heavy cedar chest
and you found the task difficult to complete
would you let someone kiss your aching forearms?
When you see your nipples poke through
your fresh white tee shirt
are you a little turned on by yourself?
Do you wear boyfriend jeans
or your boyfriend's jeans?
When you sit in a porno theater
eat a bag of m&m's and watch
the other men circle you like pacing predators
and one man stops at the end of the aisle
and rubs his crotch against an armrest
is your gender the friction of his penis in his jeans?
Are you the pocketknife you use to slice the flesh
from half-sour apples on your break from your summer hike?

Do you wish you were a red canoe?
Red water of the river?
Red rooster that attacked you on the farm as a kid
that you fended off with a shovel and a tin trash can lid?
When you get lonely after a few days alone
and hit up a guy to video chat with on the apps
and he says *oh yeah fuck yeah dude* when he comes
do you want to be the worn out tank top
he uses to wipe himself clean?
Are you the cowboy you dreamed you'd be?
Do your parents know your real name?

Natalie Tombasco

Nomenclature

Today's new words are the following: *Grass* is a mounted
video camera usually in dark alleys or near ATMs in order

to catch someone of wrongdoing :: Thankfully, because the mayor

has increased spending on *grass*, authorities were able to find
the suspect who failed to pay his subway fare. *Mountain* is a small

and heavy object of blown glass, placed upon papers to keep

from a disturbance :: *Mountains* are often collected for hobby.
Foghorn is a long commercial shown between one to six a.m.

to sell blenders and memory improvement courses :: She became

reliant upon turning on *foghorns* to find sleep. *English muffins*
have a nightmarish taste, like falling in an elevator. It doesn't matter

how much well-tempered butter is spread into the nooks

and crannies. *Stingray* is a white tablet to temporarily
eliminate sensation :: The headache was so bad, I spilled

a whole bottle of *stingrays* on the bus. *Extinction* is what

Girl Scouts go door to door selling boxes for financial literacy
and badges. *Rivers* should be hand-rolled and smoked slow

after a long day. *Rivers* are contemplative and offer sage advice.

Paradise is an antimicrobial used in the treatment
of open wounds :: Every time I scrape my knees, Momma

pours *paradise* on the cut and it burns real bad.

Bryce Berkowitz

Microwaving Sub Sandwiches in the Trailer

You'll never see poor as beautiful.
That could've been my life is what I'm saying.
That used to be my life is what I'm saying.
Some days I can't face life is what I'm saying.
Back then, green plastic paratroopers were all I knew.
I tossed them how a child tosses a football alone—
in one high arc, too close to the body—
and when they sailed to the ground,
that was the same ground where I spent
my first shell casings. Where my father's hands
wrapped my hands. Where my hands wrapped
the warm handle. Our faces disappearing
into the gray bloom of gun powder. We had
everything but money. Who are you to tell me,
Don't say please? Who are you to decide,
what's a good way of daydreaming? Who are you
to ask, *Where are you going with this?* I shouldn't
be taking so many pictures of the sky, but I am.
I can see that you think we're the same.
But where are your wings? The gravel road ends.

Nicole Caruso Garcia

Is This Your Cow?

After one hundred days learning German on Duolingo.com

Your cow is pretty. I like your shoes.
Do you like me? I bring strawberries and wine.
The garden is not beautiful.

I eat the potato because I like potatoes!
This vegetarian does not like me.

Questions are great. Is it my turn?
How many children do you have? How much wine do they drink?
Are these your pants? Either yes or no.
When is a man a man? Your oranges are big.
Why is it so small? Is that a button?

A bee!

The man is not sad. He is never sad. He drinks a lot of beer.
The man has a spider. No woman likes him.
I like him since he is paying for the food.

I do not wear any clothes. I am not wearing anything.
I am normal. I have many fans.
I am drinking and you are paying.

The beer is weak. The bear is strong.
You don't know the bear. (I know him through a friend.)

The bear is wearing her dresses. (The shoes do not fit.)

A bee!

We are not men. All women. The girls are not sad.
My tool, please. (The women like the tools.) That is not a toy.
I do not know these people. Are these your fans?
You are babies. We are playing without you.

A bee!

You are not funny. Nobody likes that.
The cat is funny. He runs as soon as he sees you.
You are weak. You are heavy. You are slow. You learn nothing.

This bed is cold. The house has no roof.
No, it is not easy.
That is not a garden.
Nobody plays.
No one speaks.
No one is good.

And if he hears you?
The enemy is weak.
We do not see the enemy.
We are running even though we are tired.
We see the trees. We see the sun.
As long as we are fast, we run.
I am alive. I know that.

Without you I am nothing. It is a garden without flowers.
The wind is cold.
We have no bread.
The sky is falling.

Su Cho

How to Say Water

Pucker your lips like a fish, your tongue
a cautious eel, pushing its head
to the roof of your mouth.

Breathe through your nose as you practice
the silence of this exercise.
Don't bite yourself

trying to make water with sounds of agreement
from your chest. Yes, that *mm*—
simultaneously creates

a small gap between those tense lips.
Tilt your head back, a finger
on your throat.

Please, start from the top and try to follow
along. I wish you could borrow
my body to say water.

This is the easiest way I can help you say 물
because I could never help my parents
say girl, ice cream, parfait.

April Freely

Every Verb is a Lesson in Longing or Dread

Dear Reader, it wouldn't be a lie if you said poetry was a cover
for my powerlessness, here, on this plane
having ticked off another day waiting for her diagnosis to rise.
As the air pressure picks up, I feel the straight road
curved by darkness, where the curve is a human limit,
where the second verb is mean, the second verb is to blind.
On the other line, my mother sits on her bed
after a terrible infection. Her voice like a wave
breaking through the receiver, when she tells me
that unlike her I revel in the inconclusivity of the body.
+
At the end of the line, I know my mother
accumulates organ-shaped pillows after surgery.
First a heart, then lungs.
The lung pillow is a fleshy-pink. The heart
pillow, a child-drawn metaphor. Both help her expectorate
the costs to the softer places of her body.
After each procedure they make her cross,
the weight of the arm comes down. These souvenirs
of miraculous stuffing other patients on the transplant floor covet,
the way one might long for a paper sack doll made by hand.
Though the stuffing is just wood shavings, one lies
with the doll tight at the crick of an elbow at night.

—Nominated by *Poem-a-Day*

Nathan Lipps

How to Believe

I've spent the day struggling
to split wood
for a fire I do not need
though I want to need it.

It's a lucky moment.
To sweat with the sun
and cold clear air.
This is how I forget

what I choose to look
away from.
With the effort of rhythm
the blade sometimes glancing

into the dirt. Which is good, too.
What I would say
where there a crowd
between each swing I won't

say now. I will earn the sweat
but not the fire.
The wood is passive in the act.
I tell myself this.

Sadia Hassan

A List of Places I Am [ ]

After Mahreen Sohail

1. Just before my birthday
    a) in a different country than the one I am from
    b) in a different country than the one in which I live

2. I am [ ]
    a) according to websites
    b) talk shows
    c) therapists

3. I feel sorry for being [ ], but they reassure me
    a) being [ ] is easy
    b) being [ ] is hard

4. In the airport, I am [ ]
    a) when I try to board a plane back to America
    b) and the Homeland Security officer wants to know what I have lost

5. I am [ ] recounting
    a) upon return that which I have lost on the train
    b) that which cannot be recovered
    c) my wallet, passport, notebook, camera
    d) my dignity, candor, care

6. At the grocery store, I am [ ]
    a) in the aisle between the baked goods and the Mexican toppings

b) when I see a man with mismatched socks the color of Jujyfruits
c) when suddenly, the doors disappear

7. I am [ ] at the counter after
    a) as I try to pay for my coffee
    b) and the cashier hands back my license in confusion

8. In class
    a) when a question is asked and I cannot bear the answer over the buzz of my body
    b) when the discussion, like so many others, goes on without me

9. At work
    a) when I ask for a moment to collect myself
    b) and the moments organize themselves against me

10. At the laundromat
    a) folding clothes between panic attacks
    b) stunned at the shadows making monsters against glass
    c) which my body reminds me could be men with knives or men with hands or men with fruit and bread with which to [ ] me

11. I am [ ]
    a) on holidays with my mother, the only person with whom I wish I were un [ ]
    b) after dinner, faces greasy with the week's earnings, the phantom memory of that night falls away, stunned still as a stone between us

12. On weekends
    a) spooning yogurt into heavy-bottomed glass
    b) making promises to be normal

13. I declare: in my new life, I will fuck
    a) open-mouthed
    b) guileless
    c) unafraid

14. For years after
    a) when my father wonders where I have been
    b) and I have been nowhere in Somali

15. I say:

16. In Somali, I am [   ]
    a) in English

17. In English, [   ]
    a) is a mistranslation of silence

18. In silence I pray for what
    a) I could not hold off
    b) I could not hold
    c) I could not
    d) I could
    e) I

—Nominated by the University of Mississippi MFA English Program

Henry Goldkamp

The Our Daddy

dead dad. hey
you. you're great.

o.k.   bring it on—
I'll do whatever you say.

            straddle the county line
& these grasses seem equally green.
                        (turn in your neighbor
            -hood rules to mine, see what happens.)

mi casa es su casa. sounds appropriate
them many selves.

give me some bread
& forgive me!
                        for all those times I *hee-haw! hee-haw!*
past   POSTED NO TRESPASSING
& don't even know what state I am in,
carrotless & drunk until empty   -   bottled at field parties.

                        I forgive people all the time.
                        I like the way they taste

& see. don't you ever fucking bring me
to the bad guys. got me?
the fuck off my property.

I believe. I be left. I bereft.
  a man.   o men.   omen.

Margaret Ray

First, and Then, and Then

We'd watched too much *Battlestar Galactica*
in the weeks leading up to the big anniversary
of the moon landing, so it seemed
like a really minor deal when it came around
and all the news outlets and search engines couldn't
let up about it. Truly impressive things happen
every day, here in the future, like the miracle
of LASIK eye surgery gone right and the lady
down the street who microchipped her dog.
Satellites clutter up the night sky, and we're still
adding to the list of things that can kill us,
but it *is* a good idea to keep thinking about how
symbolic firsts are orchestrated. I couldn't very well
have done anything other than carry myself
across the threshold of my first apartment all those years ago,
when happiness had seemed as far away as the moon,
which, it turned out, was two days by rocket and also
thousands of years of humanity staring into space.
And anyway, *carry* becomes the wrong verb
for anything other than a tune in both zero gravity
and self-sufficient womanhood. Whether we know it or not,
the world has already handed us our lines
for when we come to grief, though method acting is optional.
Me, I've been gathering reports of people
whose second lives have bent toward joy.

Look at you, here, in my life, the machine
of the world that set us in orbit together,
my astonishment undimmed by the daily sight of you
entering a room. Or the sound of your whistling
carrying through the door.

—Nominated by *The Gettysburg Review*

Tyler Starks

Walk It Off Octopus

On a day like today, I can love you forever.
Sorry for being so forward. Sorry for wrapping you up
in such a large, intense gesture. In fact, today reminds me of an afternoon
years ago, when I was in class, marine biology, which took place
in the depths of a concrete building, this damp and dark basement
simulating the bottom of the sea, and the teacher, an all-around solid guy, waxed on
and on about the individual functions for the three hearts
in an octopus, which I figured, and still believe, were all for love, which
would also explain all their tentacles hopelessly trying to get a grip
on everything passing by, and through this one window, level with the ground,
I could make out that the first hours of spring, right then,
were just kind of blowing around, and people could finally stand outside
without wanting to kill themselves, and willing to offer one another
some loose chatter, nothing too heavy, and my heart, that ridiculous
and troublesome car part, was doing some leaps in my chest, really making itself known,
and if I had three of them nothing else would ever get a word in, I mean
at that point, I'd be one giant heart machine, bumping into stuff
and when I came up for air, the teacher had, I guess, moved on
to the bacterial communities inhabiting seaweed and I'm still trying
to figure out how he had the courage to do just that.

—Nominated by Hollins University's Jackson Center for Creative Writing

Marissa Davis

Marketplace

Decade of sporadic self-starvation's MARISSA DAVIS, who should have recognized that army laying siege on her sister's mind, should have known how little air it takes to blow a girl off cliff's edge, having lived it, having kept her mama sleepless for years fearing how deep the chasm falls & the sound a daughter's body makes when its bones break ground, instead, phobic of envy & plummet, ignores each sign of sister tripping faster into savage disarray, sold to guilt & guilt by her evaporating sibling, her mother's corybantic love.

*

MARISSA DAVIS, who makes the mistake of sleeping with a man a week after Ashbery dies, cannot forget him so never reads Ashbery, excepting one poem of which the only word she can remember is *trees* & proceeds to hunt for like a white whale, as if its title were a spell for unraveling desire's cashmere straightjacket, for extracting Hell from the otherwise innocuous Dodge, by which she means the staggered heart from the body's aches it bridles, as horrified of the heart as she is of earthworms of her body as the black holes of words without translations, sold by misshapen *retrouvailles* to a summer that in its gut is winter, too.

*

September 23, 2020's MARISSA DAVIS, who, blaming cortisol & a year for breeding vultures, spends spring growing her hair in stalks just for summer to rip it out again, who envies her hair it has no mother that could miss it, that when it aches of being just jumps ship & clogs the drain, who envies, too, all the white poets writing love poems because love is something that happens to them, always to them, as expected as sunburn as expected as breath, sold by mood indigo & an all-over birthmark bullseye to each of ten frantic fingers pulling clumped coils out the pipes.

*

From Exasperated Therapist, MARISSA DAVIS, who, asked to practice making company of her own reflection, sings at a pitch to shatter all the house's glass, asked to list her favorite features says _____, asked the origin of such silence says, *idk mercury retrograde I guess?,* asked *please let's try to be serious* says *don't you know when you're not wanted*, asked what wakes her up each morning, says *there's longing on my tongue like a soggy ambrosia,* asked what this means says *some days I'd like to be a blush in a public rose garden some days just a dandelion armed with iron roots,* says *I'd trade my body for a story that would make me want the damned thing back,* says a prayer for anagnorisis, sold to a mind's eye carnival mirror by *come and see the blood in the streets come and see the blood in the streets come and see the blood in the streets*

*

MARISSA DAVIS, co-written by uncivil river & the hazy knees of Appalachia, will crack against a series of impenetrable cities, claim to grow wings despite feet that map back to the memory of stone, to the far side of thunderheads, to the prayer that a coyote's shout is enough to rearrange her mind's translucent woodlines, that a bobcat's whine might snap the dizzy out her blood & conjure back some split birthmemory, she must have held it, whatever it is the mine-gouged hills know, whatever it is river trusts even in her parents' village so forgotten you can't drink water from the tap, *what else but me can flood & fast-flow, what else can name me make me clean*, sold by an inborn phototropism to the generosity of a valley violin-bowed by dusk.

*

December 1st's MARISSA DAVIS, whose mother, to birth her, waged war with blizzard & her own barbaric blood, whose father couldn't breathe her name for weeping, whose stars, in baptizing her wanderer, blessed her with curse, or cursed her with blessing, deemed the home of her body a fate to be tripped only in search, it will not be handed to her, though for the voyage she may take from her father red willpower, from mother such tranquil rebellion, from sister how to arch eyebrows swill

Jack survive the brain's trained scratchings & be proud of being proud of being proud, preparing for when in a blaze of iron hamstring she will tear loose from the auction house, smash the locks smash the glass smash any thing that makes thing of her, sold to, sold to—

o priceless crescendo

With a line by Pablo Neruda

Jennifer Sutherland

Positioning

The geese always know where to be,
and they arrive just in time. The reindeer

are never mistaken; invariably they shed
velvet, route the necessary blood and fat

to bone and hide. A caterpillar, at exactly
the right moment, begins to generate

the imaginal cells that will become wings,
antennae, once the novice body

has swallowed and digested itself. The fish,
when the coastline changes, trusts his prerogative

to swim. He goes where the current guides him.
I have been here, a long time, without deciding.

Katelyn Botsford Tucker

House for Sale

A quiet street in a desirable neighborhood offers a lovely, three-bedroom split with big windows and a sprawling backyard. There's carpet everywhere—even the bathrooms—but it was never tacked down. An easy fix. Just pull it up. Roll it away. The showerheads are newly installed. They were put in the same day I learned the story of Bloody Mary from the girls down the street; the ones who liked to watch scary movies and play Ouija. On the kind of day that makes you avoid mirrors—just in case there's something in the glass. The wallpaper is a bit yellowed from all the smoke. You might find a stray puzzle piece. She did so many. I'm not even sure she enjoyed them. I didn't ask. What are your thoughts on almond colored Formica counters? There's a matching kitchen table, but the blue, knit carpet has a stain from the day the counter broke her fall. I knew I should have called the ambulance. She asked for scrambled eggs. One had an embryo, partially formed, with bright, red streaks. I threw it away and stared into the trash. Started over. I'm not even sure she ate.

Mandy Gutmann-Gonzalez

Sarah Good's Confession

[March 1, 1692]

From prosperity I fell: twist of wounded falcon
become stone, petrified midair, silver wing
flits first & fits fist next—is tragedy to fall
or be born down? Neither, seems; tragedy
reserved for kings. Shame to walk into
god's living room for fear I'd be thought ghoul,
his throne approaching in cloths so worn
a worm would deem it goody earth
or a garment aggravated by ten years grave, so,
nott wishing to be god's fright, I had myself
coppice-hid. But just as hunger coerces
cornered rabbit to wolfe jaw, I've seen myself
around from door to door, where bystanders
say byes with earth stuffs: rain spit, rain rocks
in my direction, and, as doors open for their
slamming pleasure, I've felt air relax into its shape
behind the banish. Ready am I to confess
my hunger: oh god have mercy on this
humble corpse which flattened low by
desperation, partook in the following mischiefs:

1. myself turned into a rabbit and ate my neighbor's lettuce,
2. myself turned into a snake and devoured my neighbor's hen eggs whole,

3. myself turned into a little girl and sucked on the teats of my neighbor's cow and drank till full,
4. myself turned into a ram, mounted my neighbor's sheep, and took the extra lambs,
5. myself turned into a pail and slurped my neighbor's butter as I churned,
6. myself turned into a goat and ate my neighbor's horse whip like jerky.

Thus I passed my hunger onto my neighbors, who
call me *unsavory* though I taste of their groceries.

Erin L. McCoy

How a Lake Flash-Froze a Herd of Horses

One bird died and one bird made it.
                    Capsules of light,
the sky sheepish. I carved my own
          ring. I mean the rain fell around
my hands on the railing. Before I knew
                    who I am with you looking,
we ground the capsules down. How those
          northern lakes groaned
                    wide as hinges. Look
how much I had. Meanwhile the horses.
          Have I told you this? Birches melting
like drools of frosting, horses with ash
                    caked on their gums saw the lake
and charged in. Cold wide uncut.
                    One bird dead and one
diminished. I tried to feed it every day.
          Have I told you this? At least one speck
of dust is a requisite catalyst
                    to freeze water. The horses, in one
instant. Since then, no one has touched them.
          They are there now, noses
flared, snorting up all the bright
                    bright bright bright   never
expelling it. You loved me this
          much. How could I keep it?

Jane Huffman

Six Revisions

The doctor holds my chest against the discus, listens like the fish below the ice listens to the fisherman. "Medicine," he says, "is not an exact science."

He listens like the ice fisherman listens to the fish. I breathe into a nebulizer and think about translation—inexact art. A fine, particulate mist.

Snow has fallen on
still-green grass,
daubed with yellow leaves.

——

Three takes on a line from St. Augustine's *Confessions*. An acquaintance posted one online to the delight of followers, of *us*, and in delight, I went to the source, the lexicon: three alike, online translators, some fishy, copied, pasted, fished out of the public sphere. And each rings like a different key.

Snow has fallen
on [yellow] grass, daubed with
[still-green] leaves.

——

Poor old pear-thief Augustine, half-biographer:

1. "Where should my heart flee to in escaping from my heart?"
2. "Where could my heart flee to in escaping from my heart." [sic]
3. "For where could my heart flee from my heart?"

[Grass] has fallen
on [still-white snow] daubed
with [yellow] leaves.

———

In the first translation is a hammering. "Should"—a moral judgment. An oiled object laid bare on a linen bed. "Shouldn't" tied around the "should" with butcher's string.

In the second, a yip, a certainty, desperate in its forwardness. "Where could?" as if the possible eluded him. To boot, denied its final mark. The thought falling from "Where could?" like rain from a cloud, a vanishing source.

Grass has fallen
on [yellow] snow daubed
with [snow-white] leaves.

———

"This will cut the cough off from the brain," the doctor says, offers me a tiny cup of codeine-orange syrup. The ache escapes like orange silk out of my orange lung. I slide into a mirror of my feelings, my face enlarged, expanding like a sponge. I grab at it.

The doctor says, "I lost it in the war." He is talking about his thumb.

[Yellow leaves have] fallen
on [white] snow daubed
with [still-green grass].

—

In the third Augustine translation is a thrum: "For / where / could / my / heart / flee / from / my / heart?" The thrum escaped the darkness of the drum. No "to" this time. The "to" escaped the darkness of the "from."

Yellow leaves have fallen
on [green grass] daubed
with still-[white snow].

Quotation sources, in order of appearance: 1. *Confessions*, translated by Henry Chadwick (Oxford University Press, 1991); 2. A misprint of the Chadwick translation, transcribed on an online resource; and 3. *Augustine of Hippo* by Peter Brown with translations by Michael Walsh (University of California Press, 1967).

Patrick James Errington

Not an Elegy

You are dead and the dead are very patient.
—Jack Spicer, *After Lorca*

Thank fuck there's still a little weather left. Snow,
Which means you don't have to talk about it, means
Despite itself, no poems needed. That said, outside

The beech trees are making metaphors for you, and
In the hallway the light seems to feel some need to fill
All the corners like water, as if some losses wouldn't be

Happy left lost. But they'll be fine, right? I mean, sure,
You still have to wear a language, like a Walmart uniform
All creases and unwashed rigid, but it doesn't mean you

Have to say anything. The words can serve themselves
For a change, wandering in the aisles, all want without
What. Of course they can't help but mean no matter

The mechanism but what's to say they have to mean
Him? Nothing, that's what; he's for the line you meant
This to be. For today, fuck it, it's snowing, stay in. Eat

Your Wheaties dry. In this sentence no one has to die.
And there's weather enough for a few more. With luck
It'll keep a while, keep up. Even if you can't help wondering

When you'll actually dig a real poem out of this. Yes, you
Know that will mean him, mean leaving the weather hollow
Like a bell. And hey, some say it's the empty part that rings.

But it's best left later. Save all that for the next draft, with
Your better metaphors, standing, half-lit in the hallway,
For everything they're not, the snow meaning wildly beyond.

That one will mean admitting him, what he is. But it's already
So late now and this poem's ending, settling into nouns like
Nothing. Someday, you'll admit *you* almost always means *me*.

Grace Wang

Zodiac Year of the Lamb

Mother, in her slight accent,
calls olives "Oliver."
She loves Oliver, brine
salty in her mouth.
Almost twenty-five years in America
and she cannot differentiate
between a man and a fruit,
but what is the difference, really?
Both are green,
hollow on the inside.
We eat until our cheeks are full
and pretend to be satisfied:
Oliver in our stomachs, something
similar to a stone, but softer,
like a half-dissolved body.
Oliver between our hips,
Mother and I buy red clothing for the winter.
She calls everything beautiful,
mispronounces the word at uneven
intervals, but says it right
when she looks at me, hair braided
into a facsimile of the girl she used to be.
You're just like me, she says.
Beautiful, like me.
She is wrong, and I never know

how to tell her.
Our lips and our throats match,
but our tongues have no relation.
Her stomach growls.
I pose for her.

Remi Recchia

Dead Name

For Frank Dubois and other "female husbands," 1883

I still turn when I hear my dead
name at the coffee shop, feel etymological
bomb spray shrapnel across the room.

A blond creature snakes her way to the front
counter, takes steamed milk & chocolate, hands
small like mine, but pretty. My knuckles have

calloused themselves since an early birth
in the early morning. Stained with bar-dust
& forever-bruises. Tar under fingernails.

My new name I bear proudly like an iguana
his jeweled robe, having shed an expired
skin. Every man will ask his wife to keep

a secret. It's up to her whether or not she'll loose
it like a rabid dog. Tabloids come at all
hours. Did Frank Dubois ever stand a chance?

His vagina sealed shut like a secret, his Gertrude
unsmiling. A hundred years later & still we believe her
when she says she didn't know.

How long does it take to suffocate
instinct? To bury billions of genes in the making,
passing name down from mother to daughter,

granddaughter from grandmother? We can barely
trace these origins but know them when we see
them. Maybe Frank's husband wouldn't have ripped

his small-town Wisconsin from Frank had he grown
hair & penis like me. Maybe no one
would have noticed. Frank, I will not print your dead

name, won't, though tempted, call your wife
coward. We didn't have the words in the Trans-
continental era, but still we hopped night

trains, swung from circus rafters, seduced near-
death experiences seconds from the tracks. Left
notes folded neatly on goose feather pillows. As a child,

I thought crime around each corner, an inevitability
from the movies I wasn't allowed to watch. I looked
for axes out of my eye-corners upon leaning my head

under the faucet for a three-a.m. tap-water gasp, convinced
the sink was a tree stump & the witch in the woods
would execute me at the neck, her blade buried in my last

wishes. But the only witch now is the hunt I'm dodging
with Frank Dubois. He's not behind or ahead, he's with me,
in me, evading this hunt without beagles or guns, French

horn transformed into the echoes of our old names, excess
syllables filling our heads while we strut on the streets
crowded with the girls & deaths we used to look like.

David Joez Villaverde

Granizo, or Apologia Pro Lustro

1. Cielo

I began a poem about Pittsburgh, thinking about how good it would be to say: *this will always be a city I left you in or when I come back you'll still be here* or I began a poem about a river winding through time where the metaphors bled together, thinking about how good it was when Satchel Paige said: *don't look back, something might be gaining on you* or I began a poem where the Monongahela became the winding streets of Coyoacán and my love was an ofrenda for someone who hadn't yet died, thinking about how good it was when יהוה said: *escape for thy life; look not behind thee* or I began a poem where I was the water—the mackled light dancing on my surface slowly becoming the white spots of a fawn, the light falling like granizo, and I thought of how Frida painted herself as a stag with nine arrows piercing her flesh or how a doe protects her young by keeping them scentless or how Hercules captured a hind with golden antlers to dedicate to Artemis and I thought about how good it would be to say: *I am sorry for the arrows, I am glad we spent this time together.*

Codex Lemniscatus

There are parts I refuse to acknowledge: the Frida Kahlo tequila I bought you when I loved another woman / the yellow roses drying in the bottle. The scent of rust thick on your neck like the costume jewelry crowding the dresser / so much of us gathering dust. Here is the glass I have sown in the fallow field of forgetting: every night I died in my sleep and every morning I woke to something less than myself. I am trying to remember the smell of burning copal / if the ash resembles a pillar of salt. I want you to tell me I'm wrong / that this admission means more than a burnt offering. I want to say: your love was more than a sachet muffling my cries

A.
La Vela

2. Tierra

In the poem the twin lunulae of the Smithfield Street Bridge represented our confluence, and I thought it would be good to say: *lenticular truss bridge* or *lemniscate curving inward* or in the poem I burned ten dollar words to avoid the serpentine memory of La Candelaria where you thought it was good to say: *me siento como una cervata atrapada o un ciervo herido*, or in the poem I tried to avoid the teeming blue of the waters which was the blue of the house or the blue of your grandmother's hair, the dark bleeding blue of the sky over the cities of the plain or in the poem the river was a brushstroke that some gringo thought good to call: *the performative aspect of indigeneity* or I was the brushstroke or I was the papier-mâché Judas with my hands on the table or Hercules chasing the hind for a full year, never slowing my pace or you were Granizo, stage left and I was La Mesa Herida with a brushstroke for a mouth that thought it good to say: *I am sorry they took your foot, I am sorry I took something much worse.*

Codex Vulneratus

You were right when you said: tus malditas amenazas de amor / hablabas mentiras que todavia no podian existir / decías promesas que desaparecian al tocar el aire / that my love was a smoke signal precipitating a battle / that I should have brought marigolds not roses. I am sorry I have left fingerprints on your retrato / bloodied your altar. I am still trying to find the right words to say: lo siento / I didn't mean to burn the sage in your boquet garni / give up as soon as you wanted to turn back. I want you to hear me say this / even if it's just the part of you I keep alive inside me / I am sorry this is the only way I can say: discúlpame / es la distancia que quema

→ B.
La Flor de
Cempasúchil

3. Mictlān

In the painting the curtains are taffeta and Frida thinks it good to say: *estoy tulliada, no muerta o mis ramas son mis ancestros y ando con la muerte* o en la pintura estás en medio del divorcio and you are no longer Lot's nameless wife, slave to a man who will go on to fuck your children or in the painting there is no palo santo and the calavera is not made of sugar but the table is covered in your blood as if it would be good to say: *vulneratus, non victus* or *I have not forgotten the trauma caused by love* or in the painting the Nayarit clay is a skirt chaser from Yucatán whose unknown blood still pumps through your open wounds or Granizo is the pan de muerto lining the altar, a sweet oblation left for the dead, or your mother is the doe who orphaned her fawn when she no longer smelled only herself on it, or this painting, lost sixty years ago, is the family portrait hanging in my parents' house, the one with you still in it, the one I am looking at now, thinking about how Hercules and Judas thought it good to say: *look at this gold, I have brought it for you.*

Kyle Carrero Lopez

After Abolition

Prisons and cops survive only in tales for the young
like twin Atlantises or two drowned boogeymen.
A cop's as harmless a Halloween getup as any
monster, while a prisoner costume's as taboo as a slave one
now that schools teach what makes them kin.
A prison is the far-off past of a structure
turned free housing, each cell wall knocked to sandcastle
ruin, halls reshaped and re-dyed in green paints,
former floor plans carved out like shores
into spacious homes, laundry and A/C a given in each.
Though prisons and cops won't be found anywhere,
our youths still learn of them, and they know what they mean,
how they look, how they function, what it will take to stop them
if they return with new names.

Jessica Lynn Suchon

Adultery

Each time the brass bell spasms,
the married man falcons the café door.
Women drift by on the sidewalk.
I think *his wife his wife his wife.*
In four months, I will turn eighteen.
He reaches across the table, grazes
my shoulder and peels a thin layer
of sunburnt skin, as if he is turning
the page of a very delicate book.

Micah Ruelle

The Last Birthday Gift

my father gave my mother
was a pistol. Small, like her.

Who did he imagine
she would have to become?

JinJin Xu

To Red Dust (II)

Mo Gao Grottoes, 1994

Two figures drawn in red dust, a woman
and a man side by side half-

submerged in the eight hundredth eighty-
eighth cave carved with Buddhas, once adorned

with prayer, adored by defaced gods. Through my flashlight
they widen, one of me, two of them, eight hundred eyes

watching as they carve their names to stone,
stroke by stroke claiming this life of theirs,

of ours, my mother, my father, drawing the outlines
of their bodies separate, together, into stone,

the singing desert air, fingertips swirl the silken mud,
presses a red thumb to my forehead, opens my mouth to—

《紅樓夢》第一回：原來是無才補天，幻形人世，被那茫茫大士渺渺真人攜入紅塵，引登彼岸的一塊頑石。

As in "Dream of the Red Chamber" (Qing Dynasty): *When the goddess mended the hole in the sky, she left a single stone untouched / Through red dust, the monk leads the stone onto land into the form of a human.*

HongKong, 2019

A shriek: teargas, Molotov cocktails
flying through the risen sidewalk, chants

falling through our bodies like glass, as if words
will save us from demise, we step into the steaming streets

snap off our masks & are blinded—I cannot see my hands
dipping the ladle in oil, lifting it high above our heads,

to pour gently-gently like a mother bathing her newborn,
as if our bodies are made for nothing holier,

oil trickling down our foreheads, cheeks, necks,
we dab the crease of our eyes dry,

flicker of blue light,
we set our bodies into flight—

《西都賦》（東漢）：闐城溢郭，旁流百廛。紅塵四合，煙雲相連。

As in "Poem of West Capital" (Han Dynasty): *City overflowing with people / over pour of a hundred shelters / red dust rising from all four corners/ smoke and clouds merge.*

Shanghai, 2005

Of red dust, my father says, wiping away perspiration
on the car window, *your eyes will pierce through*

these earthly worries, there is no past,
no future, telephone poles flash past us

like limbs outstretched in barren rice fields,
I look at my father,

my spine loosens its anchor,
What about me?

As if I am not of my father's body, I write
my name into my exhale, *Please—*

a swipe of his palm—
Do not leave us in the red dust—

看破紅塵：來自道家自然無為的觀念。士人厭倦虛幻的官場生涯，嚮往自由、隱遁山野。

As in Taoist saying *for sight to pierce red dust*: when scholars tire of the smoke and glamour of the palace and long to retreat into nature.

baidu.com, 2019

紅塵： Red Dust

李唐王朝：盛世之下的長安車水馬龍，夕陽下捲起的西北黃土成為紅色。

As in Tang Dynasty's northwest capital, the earth was yellow. The dust raised by people and chariots turn red under the setting sun.

這個世間紛紛擾擾的世俗生活。

As in of this earthly life.

形容女子一身紅塵指她擁有豐富的人生閱歷，不專指感情。

As in a woman cloaked in red dust, meaning her body is of experience.

看破紅塵：心胸寬闊、包容萬物、寬恕眾生。若執迷於對錯得失，將無法從紅塵中解脫。

As in *for sight to pierce red dust*: to have a heart that embraces everything, forgives all things living.
To see the faults of the living is to taint yourself, to continue to live in red dust.

[ ], 2018

If you are alive, know that I am writing to
hold on, though writing is the very crime

you are charged for. Do you have a window?
Water? Any question I ask is inadequate.

My father says to forget you, to leave it all in red dust,
but they are lashing your flesh, your eyes,

and I am still alive, *hold on,*
I beg, as if I know what this earth is made of

falling to dust between my fingers,
as if I know why we cling to this life

amidst the eight hundred watchful eyes
and I am still alive and I am still—

Shanghai, [   ]

Alive, two figures drawn in red dust,
one turns to me, holds a finger to my lips

shh—do not speak of such things,
the other shuts my eyes as the screen

flashes with students, aflame,
monks, aflame, crushed into static, as if

their lives never existed, as if
all bodies return to dust—flip the channel,

we are on the mountain of eternity, my mother &
my father eating fresh peaches, red snappers suckling our toes,

I shall not speak of such things,
I shall not see & I shall not speak—

鳩摩羅什：一切都有為法，如夢幻氣泡，如露亦如電，應作如是觀。
As in the words of Kumārajīva: *All phenomena of the self are like dreams and bubbles. / Like dew and lightning. And should be perceived as such.*

[ ], [ ]

超脫紅塵：蓮之出淤泥而不染。
As in *to transcend red dust*: in the silt, a pale lotus opening.

And another alights on the sidewalk,
another alights, I step around their outlines

into our next life—*om mani padme hum*
you emerge from the red dawn to shake open my life,

upside down, flying dust, you unlock
the red cell, cameras light up one by one

like lanterns, you dig your nails into this life,
half moons of dirt, rings around my lips, *om mani padme hum*—

om mani padme hum, I am speaking in tongues,
I am spitting out my lungs, I want to howl your name

across the headlines, carry your body over the threshold
of holy until words are just words and sight is just sight,

nothing worth dying for.

—Nominated by the New York University Creative Writing Program

Adam J. Gellings

Second Person

You know how to spend what
little time you have: what little time you will always have.

You will always have what little you want. What little
you want. You know how to repeat.

You know when the time is right to create
distance—You know how to cover ground?

Covering ground is what you want.
You know how to live when the dogs are barking.

You know when they bite. You know
how to let teeth shaped like small vessels sink

into your arms. A bite mark is sometimes what you
want. You know how to slowly walk them back

to the yards where they belong. You
mostly know how to belong. You

know the cavernous & you
know the fields. You know

miserable things that burrow & reappear.
To burrow & reappear is mostly what you want.

Come, tell me there is nothing you can't hide behind.

Mary Ardery

Fourth-Grade Soundtrack

Starting that January, my father's meeting
          met in our living room.

My parents prepared each Thursday
          after dinner—a pot of coffee brewing

as my mother peeled open a package of Oreos,
          then helped my father

drag the kitchen chairs into a circle.
          When a friend's mother dropped me off

after volleyball practice, cars lined our driveway.
          They parked bumper to bumper,

connected like a strand of dark Christmas lights
          waiting to be plugged in. Inside,

my mother stood at the top of the stairs,
          one finger pressed against her lips—

a tiny crucifix of flesh—reminding me
          not to let the front door slam.

After I showered, she tucked me in
    but I could still hear the voices

of the men below. A low soothing rumble
    like the white noise of an engine,

an occasional laugh, and at the end,
    a chorus of chairs scraping hardwood

before the sounds of my father cleaning up.
    Brief rush of the kitchen faucet,

then the rinsed coffee pot fitting back into its divot.
    The lock turned in the front door

and my father's slow footsteps on the stairs,
    steady enough to walk a straight line

and touch his index finger to the tip of his nose.

Chris Crowder

On the Street Marked "Dead End"

Tree shadows make a long barcode.
With the old shoes I reserve for outside and my hairline
like the edge of a tide, I drag through the earth,

next to the cornhusks, a torn-up bag of Miracle-Gro,
a pile of feathers from a dove, mounds of horse shit
covered in sawdust, a white fence checkered with pink roses
next to a fuzzy brown horse after it rains,
stomped-on worms writhing in their own slime,
and a goose you can never look at in the eye—

everything on a hill, round like a belly can feel.

I pick up a worm, ask it why it's on the road.
Hail-dented cars nearly hit both of us. Things
are always being born. In every instance of *right now,*
someone is learning how to survive. My parents

tell me to never say that the world is crazy. Rather,
we inherit muscle memories and recipes for how to deal

with the latest definition of *the worst.* Lord, I haven't seen
another Black person in weeks. I haven't been to a good cookout

in a minute. But I remember how it smells. And I remember speakers
blasting "Knuck If You Buck," which pumps me up to tell the sun

to fuck off. Because lately, I've only seen that star in the middle
of the sky. Lately, I've guessed wrong. If it will go down or up.

huiying b. chan

how we survived: 爺爺's pantoum (i)

In 1973 my grandfather made a five-mile swim from Shenzhen Bay to Hong Kong, across shark-filled waters guarded by the People's Liberation Army. He was part of an exodus of hundreds of thousands who fled from Guangdong as refugees of the Cultural Revolution. This is his story.

you had to know the currents, & the sun
stay shallow to keep warm in the waters.
you had to believe you could do it
& not be afraid to die.

stay shallow to keep warm in the waters
dream of banyan roots aglow
i was not afraid of dying
even as tides surged my blued lips.

i dreamed of banyan roots aglow
when pistol shots scraped shoreline
tides surged my blued lips
toisan frog treading to freedom.

when pistol shots scraped shoreline
i cried out for my hing dai
toisan frogs treading to freedom
trachea inflamed, violet balloon.

i cried out for my hing dai
when searchlights flooded our vision
tracheas inflamed, violet balloons
liberation army cuffed us soon.

when searchlights flooded our vision
i pretended the sun was rising
liberation army cuffed us soon.
record that in this pantoum.

i pretended the sun was rising
when rocks scraped scalps & wood splintered knees
record that in this pantoum.
i waited for the scars, & returned.

rock-scraped scalp & wood-splintered knees
bandaged in 嬤嬤's scolds, congee, & lotus root
i waited for the scars, & returned
new hing dai came searching for a guide.

bandaged in 嬤嬤's scolds, congee, & lotus root
i trained laps in the bay each night fall
new hing dai came searching for a guide
water lilies & crickets, our witness.

we trained laps in the bay each nightfall
i had to believe we could make it
water lilies & crickets, my witness
this time, i knew the currents & the sun.

for 爺爺
in memoriam

爺爺 — yeh yeh, Cantonese for paternal grandfather
嬤嬤 — mah mah, Cantonese for paternal grandmother
hing dai — Cantonese for brothers or close friends

Augusta Funk

Poem in My Mother's Voice

I was given some horses. And the horses carried
my body from the playground to the war and back again.
They must have passed through my life as children,
the men who ran ahead of me, dropping like small animals
who had grown smaller and more furious with each bullet
or number on a die. Otherwise I was cared for, was given
gloves against the rain and made to garden along the road.
I was nowhere. Flickering mountain passes. Trucks sliding
to the left and right. In my father's voice I said get out.
Never mind I was given some horses. Lightbulbs apples
glasses of sweet tea. I worked for a man who wrote
his name on everything. And the horses stood in a field
across from the hospital where I taught you to hold a fork
in your left hand while cutting, in your right while bringing food
to your mouth. You were born between roads that were
never yours. Crayons and magazines, cut-out snowflakes
and paper gowns. You were given some horses, some roads.

Gavin Yuan Gao

Myth, or Luck as a Swan Boat

Fear fear, shriek the unseen cicadas in a borrowed
language all summer long. It forms a pattern:

the cut diamond of their chorus shredding air
into thin ribbons of heat. An abandoned fountain

dry as the loins of any stone cherub. I go where
chance takes me, or is it luck—that sun-bleached

swan boat steered by nothing but the lake's caprice
through the knot of shadows cast by a willow grove.

That shadow play of *mind : foliage : mind : foliage*
until the water turns murky as unanswered prayers—

chance, a codeword for surrender; prayers, a prelude
to trust. I lie down beside the rock worn to myth

by the lake's ancient murmurs. The boat I came in
has turned to a swan, the swan now saunters towards me

as a god. Fear ebbs from me in ripples tainted by the moon
as I seek that rare kind of tenderness that lies between *rescue*

and *ruin*, guiding the god's feathered touch over the ivory
magnolia of my belly, steering his calloused hands over

mine, saying, *Here are the oars. Here is the impossible rowing.*

Hannah Perrin King

Transcript of My Mother's Sleeptalk: Chincoteague

Was not a one-trick pony.
Was the trick of many ponies.
Was the trick of swimming
The ponies from the island
To the mainland. *So as not*
To burden the island, said
The saltwater cowboys whose
Trick it was to auction off
The ponies at the pony auctions
To the women clutching their kiss-
Clasp bags of tricks. Was not
A dirt-trick island, but was
The island, was its vow to sugar
The ponies until there was
No cane left to sweeten them.
A simple trick, to die like
An island, parched, fenced in
By water, acre graveyard of
Pebbles and hooves. Oh, was
I ever a ponyless girl
On the bone-shrill island,
Was I ever a girl, was I
Asked the girl that was as
Many tricks as there were
Men, as many men as it took

To no longer be a girl. Trick was
To refuse the pony's love, to love
Instead the glue. Was I yours
The ponies asked the girl, salt caking
Their horse-long faces. Was
A girl, answered the girl. Was
What I had to be. Was the
Auction, the swam-sick
Channel. Was the grief of salt
Split open by water, of
Velvet balding under a
Bridle. Was the island of
Burden that is the girl's, burden
Of the saddle beneath the
Burden of men. Was
The night's tinfoil raft, its
Splintered, old-dog light.
Was mine, was enough.

Hannah Matheson

Daniel Johnston

sang that whole summer, said since junior high
when he lost his mind he's been *trying*
to make sense out of scrambled eggs

and I, high school punk, late-stage nerd
perfumed by an overactive limbic
system, pledged fealty to melancholy,

nodded *damn straight*, like
I'd ever had to know anything
in my life. The drive to dogsitting

felt like a secret: the eggshell horizon
leaking albumen of weak-knuckled light,
an orange suffocation, the old lab

wheezing around those June mornings.
I don't know how to explain this—
how when I look back at those months

everything was steamed dogshit,
bleaching grass, night buffering into
daybreak, the headache of waking,

watching *Friday Night Lights*
until my eyes closed against their will,
Matt Saracen's cheekbones, my sweaty thighs

splayed on beige pleather, the stereo, never
getting out of bed, the stereo, Daniel Johnston
on the stereo saying *I have to live*

these songs forever. That old lab,
I'd hardly let him pee before I'd go
again, and I couldn't stand it—

his arthritic vigil at the door when I arrived,
his ecstatic drool, then his panting as
I walked out, the asthma of being left.

Is it ok to tell you this? Sometimes
I thought sadness would kill me.
You know, don't you? The nausea

of dawn. The not-dead-yet
man's song playing as you leave
the thing too lonely to love.

Rebecca Zweig

This Poem Has a One-Night Stand

I was a street kid, I was always in the street. Do you know who Gloria Anzaldúa is? She's from my town. I didn't really know her until recently and then I had kind of a meltdown. Like this woman wrote my whole childhood before I lived it, she rotated and articulated it like a dead star. Infinite and compact. But yeah we were always on our bikes. These kids would steal the most insane things, theft was a grammatical possibility agitating the end of history, the shopping center they'd constructed around us. Like puppies. They'd steal puppies from someone's fenced-in yard and be like "oh we found them on the side of the road, can we keep them?" to their parents. Now when I visit my mom, I see versions of myself walking their bikes along the side of the highway and I always call to them like "hey you you're gonna get through it never give up you fucking dummy!" En unas pocas centurias, the future will belong to you, fucking dummy, because the future depends on the breaking down of paradigms. My sister, all she remembers is the brick house. Not the trailer or the shitty apartment or even the nice apartment. And my dad's other kids in Guanajuato don't know anything besides

experiencing human history through conflicts of weather and libido. But no they don't know what it's like to have to clean up after yourself or be left alone at night to translate from one world to the exact same world. I guess people criticize Anzaldúa for that thing with José Vasconcelos, since she got the idea for mestizaje from him and he said a mixture of races accomplished according to the laws of social well-being, sympathy, and beauty will lead to the creation of a type infinitely superior to all that have previously existed, fucking dummy. Until now reproduction has been accomplished in the manner of beasts, with no limit in quantity and no aspiration for improvement, fucking dummy. That part's yikes, blinking like a speed trap in her text. But my mom always says how I was such a good baby, how I never asked for anything. At the grocery store I'd stare hard at the coco puffs but never got mad that she couldn't buy them, since they had already been / revealed to me / while I wheeled with eternal Gemini // But I'm talking too much about myself I want to know about you are you gonna be a good girl tonight? Hand on thigh. The patio's   datura   entwines a low live wire. Is it time to leave? No it's   time to leave.
Y   es   I'll be   a good girl.

Acknowledgments

Bryce Berkowitz's "Microwaving Sub Sandwiches in the Trailer" previously appeared in *The Missouri Review.*

Kyle Carrero Lopez's "After Abolition" previously appeared in *The Nation.*

Su Cho's "How to Say Water" previously appeared in *New England Review.*

Caitlin Cowan's "Miscarry" previously appeared in *The Rumpus.*

Chris Crowder's "On the Street Marked "Dead End"" previously appeared in Poetry Foundation's *The VS Podcast.*

Tarik Dobbs's "Dragphrasis: Alexis Mateo Calls Home the Troops with a Death Drop" previously appeared in *American Poetry Review.*

Patrick James Errington's "Not an Elegy" previously appeared in *Narrative.*

April Freely's "Every Verb Is a Lesson" previously appeared in the Academy of American Poets' *Poem-a-Day.*

Augusta Funk's "Poem in My Mother's Voice" previously appeared in *Alaska Quarterly Review.*

Gavin Yuan Gao's "Myth, or Luck as a Swan Boat" previously appeared in *Parentheses Journal.*

Nicole Caruso Garcia's "Is This Your Cow?" previously appeared in *Sonora Review.*

Adam J. Gellings's "Second Person" previously appeared in *Magma Poetry*.

Henry Goldkamp's "The Our Daddy" previously appeared in *Fourteen Hills*.

Mandy Gutmann-Gonzalez's "Sarah Good's Confession" previously appeared in *Quarterly West*.

Jane Huffman's "Six Revisions" previously appeared in *Poetry*.

Katherine Hur's "Nineteen Sixty-Three: Year of the Rabbit" previously appeared in *The Southern Review*.

Zebulon Huset's "[Start at the Beginning]" previously appeared in *Gulf Stream*.

Hannah Perrin King's "Transcript of My Mother's Sleeptalk: Chincoteague" previously appeared in *The Georgia Review*.

Lauren Licona's "the first creation story i ever heard" previously appeared in *Muzzle Magazine*.

Sharon Lin's "An Offering at the Altar" previously appeared in *Sine Theta*.

Aaron Magloire's "In Which I Travel to Alternate Dimensions in Search of Healing After Another Black Man is Shot by Police" previously appeared in *Quarterly West*.

Kristina Martino's "All I Can Have Are Field Recordings of the Field" previously appeared in the Academy of American Poets' *Poem-a-Day*.

Hannah Matheson 's "Daniel Johnson" previously appeared in *The Adroit Journal*.

Erin L. McCoy's "How a Lake Flash-Froze a Herd of Horses" previously appeared in *Rougarou*.

Nancy Miller Gomez's "Siren Song" previously appeared in *New Ohio Review*.

Alicia Rebecca Myers's "Winter Solstice" previously appeared in *Threadcount*.

Karisma Price's "My Phone Autocorrects 'Nigga' to 'Night'" previously appeared in *Poetry*.

Margaret Ray's "First, and Then, and Then" previously appeared in *The Gettysburg Review*.

Caitlin Roach's "Derivations" previously appeared in *Denver Quarterly*.

Micah Ruelle's "The Last Birthday Gift" previously appeared in *Cultural Daily*.

Samyak Shertok's "No Rhododendron" previously appeared in *Colorado Review*.

Tyler Starks's "Walk It Off Octopus" previously appeared on *poets.org*.

Jennifer Sutherland's "Positioning" previously appeared in *I-70 Review*.

Katelyn Botsford Tucker's "House for Sale" previously appeared in *Second Chance Lit*.

David Joez Villaverde's "Granizo, or Apologia Pro Lustro" previously appeared in *Frontier Poetry*.

Grace Wang's "Zodiac Year of the Lamb" previously appeared in *The Adroit Journal* and *Hunger Mountain*.

JinJin Xu 's "To Red Dust (II)" previously appeared in *The Common* and the Poetry Society of America.

Contributors' Notes

MARY ARDERY is originally from Bloomington, Indiana. Her work appears or is forthcoming in *Missouri Review*'s "Poem of the Week," *Fairy Tale Review*, *Prairie Schooner*, *Poet Lore*, and elsewhere. She holds an MFA from Southern Illinois University–Carbondale, where she won an Academy of American Poets Prize. Currently, she lives in West Lafayette, Indiana, and works at the public library. You can visit her at maryardery.com.

BRYCE BERKOWITZ is the winner of the Austin Film Festival's 2021 AMC Pilot Award. He is the author of *Bermuda Ferris Wheel*, winner of the 42 Miles Press Poetry Award (forthcoming). His writing has appeared in *Best New Poets 2017*, *New Poetry from the Midwest 2019*, *The Sewanee Review*, *The Missouri Review*, and other publications. He teaches at Butler University. For more, please visit www.bryceberkowitz.com.

KYLE CARRERO Lopez was born to Cuban parents in northern New Jersey. He co-founded LEGACY, a production collective by and for Black queer artists. His work is published in *The Nation*, *TriQuarterly*, and *The Atlantic*, as well as anthologized in *The BreakBeat Poets Volume IV: LatiNEXT* (Haymarket Books, 2020) and *Best of the Net*. He holds an MFA in poetry from New York University.

HUIYING B. CHAN is a visionary poet, cultural organizer, and educator born and raised on Lenape Land (Brooklyn, New York). His work speaks to the intersections of race, gender, migration, and intergenerational healing. huiying has received fellowships from the Asian American Writers' Workshop, Kundiman, Poetry Foundation, VONA /Voices, DreamYard, and elsewhere. huiying is currently pursuing an MFA in poetry at Rutgers University–Newark, where he is working on a manuscript that excavates self-remembrance, matrilineal legacies, and queer and trans lineages. huiying's work is published in *The Margins*, *The Offing*, *Seventh Wave Magazine*, and the *Asian American Journal of Psychology*. You can connect with him online at huiyingbchan.com.

Su Cho is a poet, essayist, and editor. She's the author of the forthcoming poetry collection *The Symmetry of Fish* (Penguin Books, 2022) selected by Paige Lewis for the 2021 National Poetry Series. She is a visiting assistant professor at Franklin & Marshall College and served as guest editor and consulting editor for *Poetry*.

Born and raised in metro Detroit, Caitlin Cowan earned a PhD in English from the University of North Texas and an MFA in creative writing from the New School in New York City before returning to the Midwest. Her poetry, fiction, and nonfiction have appeared in *The Rumpus*, *New Ohio Review*, *Missouri Review*, *SmokeLong Quarterly*, and *The Rappahannock Review*, among other outlets. Her work has received support from the Hambidge Center for Creative Arts, the Sewanee Writers' Conference, and elsewhere. Caitlin has taught writing at UNT, Texas Woman's University, and Interlochen Center for the Arts. She is the associate poetry editor for *Pleiades* and serves as the chair of creative writing at Blue Lake Fine Arts Camp. You can find her at caitlincowan.com.

Chris Crowder is a poet from Flint, Michigan. He's a Zell Postgraduate Fellow in the Helen Zell Writers' program at the University of Michigan and a poetry editor for *The Adroit Journal*. His poetry has appeared or is forthcoming in *TriQuarterly*, *Zone 3*, and the *VS* podcast.

Marissa Davis is a poet and translator from Paducah, Kentucky, now residing in Brooklyn, New York. Her poetry has appeared or will soon appear in *Poem-a-Day*, *Glass*, *Frontier Poetry*, *Nimrod*, *Great River Review*, *Southeast Review*, *Rattle*, *West Branch*, *Mississippi Review*, and *Muzzle Magazine*, among others. Her translations are published or forthcoming in *Massachusetts Review*, *New England Review*, *Mid-American Review*, *The Common*, *Rhino*, and *American Chordata*, and she served as a judge for the 2021 PEN Award for Poetry in Translation. Her chapbook, *My Name & Other Languages I Am Learning How to Speak* (Jai-Alai Books, 2020), was selected by Danez Smith for Cave Canem's 2019 Toi Derricotte and Cornelius Eady Prize. Davis holds an MFA from New York University. Her website is marissa-davis.com.

Tarik Dobbs is a writer and artist born in Dearborn, Michigan, on stolen land of the Chippewa, Ottawa, and Potawatomi people. Dobbs's poems appear in *American Poetry Review*, *Best of the Net*, and *Poetry*. Dobbs's poetry chapbook, *Dancing on the Tarmac*, was selected by Gabrielle Calvocoressi (Yemassee, 2021). Find them on Twitter: @mxrlevant.

Poems by PATRICK JAMES ERRINGTON appear widely in journals and anthologies, including *The Poetry Review*, *The Iowa Review*, *Boston Review*, *Harvard Review*, *The Cincinnati Review*, *Copper Nickel*, and *Oxford Poetry*, as well as in two chapbooks, *Glean* (2018) and *Field Studies* (2019). His work has also received numerous prizes, including most recently the 2020 Poetry International Prize and the 2020 Callan Gordon Award from the Scottish Book Trust. Raised in Alberta, Canada, Patrick now lives in Scotland where he is a Teaching and Research Fellow at the University of Edinburgh.

APRIL FREELY passed away unexpectedly in July 2021. At the time, she was the executive director of the Fire Island Artist Residency. She was also a professor at Bard College in Annandale-on-Hudson, New York, and was the recipient of a 2020–21 Queer Arts Mentorship fellowship in literature, as well as receiving awards from the Ohio Arts Council, the Fine Arts Work Center in Provincetown, the Rona Jaffe Foundation, the Tulsa Artist Fellowship, and the CUE Art Foundation. Her work appeared in the *American Poetry Review*, *Ninth Letter*, *Gulf Coast*, *Kenyon Review*, and elsewhere.

AUGUSTA FUNK has received fellowships from the Bread Loaf Environmental Writers' Conference, Vermont Studio Center, and the Helen Zell Writers' Program. Her poems have appeared in *Poetry Daily*, *The Massachusetts Review*, *The Offing*, *Colorado Review*, *Alaska Quarterly Review*, *Four Way Review*, *Cream City Review*, *The Journal*, *Tupelo Quarterly*, and *The Cortland Review*. Originally from Ohio, she divides her time between Montana and California, where she is a PhD student in English at UC–Davis. You can read more of her work at augustafunk.wordpress.com.

GAVIN YUAN GAO is a poet based in Brisbane, Australia. Their work has appeared or is forthcoming in *New England Review*, *The Cincinnati Review*, *The Journal*, *Foundry*, *The Offing*, and elsewhere. They are the winner of the 2020 Thomas Shapcott Poetry Prize. Their first book of poetry, *At the Altar of Touch*, is forthcoming from University of Queensland Press.

Nicole Caruso Garcia is the author of *Oxblood* (Able Muse Press, 2022), which was named a finalist for the Able Muse Book Award and the Richard Wilbur Award for Poetry. Her poems have appeared in *DIAGRAM*, *Crab Orchard Review*, *Light*, *Measure*, *Mezzo Cammin*, *ONE ART*, *The Orchards*, *PANK*, *Plume*, *The Raintown Review*, *Rattle*, *RHINO*, *Sonora Review*, *Spillway*, *Tupelo Quarterly*, and elsewhere. She is a recipient of a fellowship to Connecticut Writing Project's Invitational Summer Institute at Fairfield University, a scholarship to the West Chester University Poetry Conference, and the Willow Review Award. She serves as associate poetry editor at *Able Muse* and an advisory board member at Poetry by the Sea: A Global Conference. Visit her at nicolecarusogarcia.com.

Adam J. Gellings is a poet and instructor from Columbus, Ohio. His previous work has appeared in *DIALOGIST*, *The Louisville Review*, *Willow Springs*, and elsewhere.

Henry Goldkamp performs his life in New Orleans. Work appears in *Yemassee*, *Tilted House*, *Denver Quarterly*, *Seneca Review*, *Idaho Review*, *New South*, the *minnesota review*, and *DIAGRAM*, among others. See the clown play himself at henrygoldkamp.com.

Nancy Miller Gomez's work has appeared or is forthcoming in *Best American Poetry 2021*, *Shenandoah*, *River Styx*, *The Rumpus*, *Massachusetts Review*, *American Life in Poetry*, *Verse Daily*, and elsewhere. Her chapbook, *Punishment*, was published in 2018 by *Rattle*. She has worked as an attorney and a TV producer and currently lives in Santa Cruz, California, where she co-founded an organization that provides poetry workshops to incarcerated women and men. She received her MFA from Pacific University. More at nancymillergomez.com

Boston Gordon is a poet from Philadelphia, Pennsylvania. They are the founder and curator of You Can't Kill A Poet, a reading series that highlights queer and transgender poets in Philadelphia. For this work, they received a Leeway Foundation Art and Change Grant in 2017. Their poetry can be found in places such as *PRISM International*, *Guernica*, and *American Poetry Review*. They have a chapbook forthcoming from Harbor Editions in 2022.

Mandy Gutmann-Gonzalez, a poet and novelist from Vilches, Chile, is the author of the novel *La Pava*, published by the Chilean press Ediciones Inubicalistas. They hold an MFA in poetry from Cornell University. Winner of the 2018 Boulevard Emerging Poets Prize, their poetry has appeared or is forthcoming in *West Branch*, *DIAGRAM*, *Quarterly West*, *diode*, *Interim*, and other literary journals. They live in Worcester, Massachusetts, and teach creative writing at Clark University. You can learn more about their work on their website: mandygutmanngonzalez.com.

Sadia Hassan is the author of *Enumeration* (Akashic Books, 2020), part of the *New-Generation African Poets: A Chapbook Set*. Hassan has received fellowships from Hedgebrook, The Bread Loaf Writers Conference, and the Mesa Refuge. Winner of the 2021 Georgia Review Emerging Writer's Fellowship, the 2020 Hurston/Wright College Writers Award, and 2019 finalist for The Krause Essay Prize, Hassan currently writes and teaches in Oxford, Mississippi, where she is pursuing her MFA at the University of Mississippi. More of her work can be found in *The Georgia Review*, *The American Academy of Poetry*, *Boston Review*, *Longreads*, and elsewhere.

Jane Huffman's poems have appeared in *Poetry*, *The New Yorker*, *The Kenyon Review*, and elsewhere. She is a 2021 Gregory Djanikian Scholar, and she was a 2019 recipient of the Ruth Lilly and Dorothy Sargent Rosenberg Fellowship from the Poetry Foundation. Jane is a graduate of the Iowa Writers' Workshop. She is founder and editor-in-chief of *Guesthouse* (www.guesthouselit.com), an online literary journal.

Katherine Hur is a Korean American writer from Atlanta, Georgia. Her poetry has appeared in *The Southern Review*, and she was the winner of *Black Warrior Review*'s 2020 Nonfiction Contest. She is currently at work on her first novel.

Zebulon Huset is a teacher, writer, and photographer. He won the Gulf Stream 2020 Summer Poetry Contest and his writing has appeared in *Meridian*, *The Southern Review*, *Fence*, *Gone Lawn*, *North American Review*, *The Texas Review*, and many others. He publishes the writing prompt blog *Notebooking Daily*, and edits the journals *Coastal Shelf* and *Sparked*.

HANNAH PERRIN KING is most recently the winner of *The Georgia Review's* 2020 Loraine Williams Poetry Prize chosen by Ilya Kaminsky. She is also the winner of *Narrative Magazine*'s Eleventh Annual Poetry Contest, as well as AWP's Kurt Brown Prize for Poetry and *New Millennium Writings'* 48th New Millennium Award for Poetry. King's work has appeared in *The Adroit Journal, Narrative Magazine, The Missouri Review, The Cincinnati Review, The Georgia Review, North American Review,* and *THRUSH,* among others. Her first manuscript is a National Poetry Series Finalist, and she received a Tin House Summer Workshop Scholarship. King originally harks from rural California and now makes her home in Brooklyn, New York.

LAUREN LICONA is a Latine poet based in Boston. Her work can be found in Poets.org, *Muzzle Magazine, diode, The Acentos Review,* and elsewhere. She is a graduate of Emerson College.

SHARON LIN is an essayist and poet. She is the author of *Electric Heart* (Ghost City Press, 2021) and is supported by the Mendocino Coast Writers' Conference and Writers House Pittsburgh. A Fulbright Fellow, recipient of the Robert A. Boit Prize, and the 2017 New York City Youth Poet Laureate, her work appears in *The New York Review of Books, The Adroit Journal, Sine Theta, Bloomsbury,* and elsewhere. She lives in Brooklyn, New York.

NATHAN LIPPS lives and works in the Midwest. His work as appeared in *EcoTheo Review, North American Review, Third Coast, TYPO,* and elsewhere.

AARON MAGLOIRE is from Queens and is a junior at Yale University, where he studies English and African-American Studies. You can find him on Instagram as @a.magloire.

KRISTINA MARTINO is a poet and visual artist. Her poems have appeared in The Academy of American Poets' *Poem-a-Day, Interim, Bennington Review, Sonora Review, Memorious, Yalobusha Review, Best New Poets 2017,* and elsewhere. She has received an MFA from The Iowa Writers' Workshop, and fellowships from The Atlantic Center for the Arts, The Studios at Mass Moca, and The Corporation of Yaddo. Some of her drawings can be viewed at kristinamartino.com.

Hannah Matheson is an MFA candidate in poetry at New York University, where she is a poetry editor of *Washington Square Review*. Previously awarded scholarships to attend The Frost Place Conference on Poetry, Hannah has work appearing or forthcoming in *Four Way Review*, *The Adroit Journal*, *Pigeon Pages*, *Solar*, *Image Journal*, and elsewhere. Hannah currently works as publicist and editor at Four Way Books.

Erin L. McCoy has published poetry and fiction in *Conjunctions*, *Pleiades*, *Narrative*, *West Branch*, and other journals. She holds an MFA in creative writing and an MA in Hispanic literature from the University of Washington. Her poem "Futures" was selected by Natalie Diaz for *Best New Poets 2017*. She won second place in the 2019–2020 Rougarou Poetry Contest, judged by CAConrad, and is currently a finalist for the *Missouri Review*'s 2021 Miller Audio Prize. Her website is erinlmccoy.com. She is from Louisville, Kentucky.

Yvette R. Murray is a Gullah poet and writer from Charleston, South Carolina. She has been published in *Emrys Journal*, *The Petigru Review*, *Catfish Stew*, *A Gathering Together*, *Call and Response Journal*, and others. She is a 2020 Watering Hole Fellow and a 2019 Pushcart Prize nominee. She is a board member of the Poetry Society of South Carolina and the South Carolina Writer's Association. Find her on Twitter @MissYvettewrites.

Alicia Rebecca Myers holds an MFA in poetry from New York University, where she was the recipient of a Goldwater Teaching Fellowship. Her poetry and nonfiction have been published in *Creative Nonfiction*, *FIELD*, *The Rumpus*, *Fairy Tale Review*, *American Literary Review*, *Gulf Coast*, and *Brain, Child Magazine*. Her chapbook of poems, *My Seaborgium* (Brain Mill Press, 2016), was selected as a winner of the inaugural Mineral Point Chapbook Series.

Karisma Price is the author of the forthcoming poetry collection *I'm Always so Serious* (Sarabande Books, 2023). Her work has appeared in *Poetry*, *Four Way Review*, *Wildness*, *The Adroit Journal*, and elsewhere. She has received fellowships from Cave Canem and New York University, was a finalist for the 2019 Manchester Poetry Prize, and awarded the 2020 J. Howard and Barbara M.J. Wood Prize from The Poetry Foundation. She is from New Orleans, Louisiana, and holds an MFA in poetry from New York University. She is currently a visiting assistant professor of poetry at Tulane University.

MARGARET RAY grew up in Gainesville, Florida. She is the author of *Superstitions of the Mid-Atlantic* (2021, selected by Jericho Brown for the 2020 Poetry Society of America Chapbook Fellowship Prize). Her poems have been published in *Threepenny Review*, *Narrative*, *The Gettysburg Review*, *Poet Lore*, *Gulf Coast*, *Michigan Quarterly Review*, and elsewhere. She is a winner of the Third Coast Poetry Prize, and her debut full-length manuscript has been a finalist for the Georgia Poetry Prize, and a semi-finalist for both the University of Wisconsin's Brittingham and Felix Pollak Prizes in Poetry and Ohio State's Charles B. Wheeler Prize in Poetry. She holds an MFA from Warren Wilson College and teaches in New Jersey. You can find her (occasionally) on twitter @mbrrray, or read more of her work at www.margaretbray.com

REMI RECCHIA is a trans poet and essayist from Kalamazoo, Michigan. He is a PhD candidate in creative writing at Oklahoma State University. He currently serves as an associate editor for the *Cimarron Review*. A three-time Pushcart Prize nominee, Remi's work has appeared or will soon appear on Poets.org and in *Columbia Online Journal*, *Harpur Palate*, and *Juked*, among others. He holds an MFA in poetry from Bowling Green State University. Remi is the author of *Quicksand/Stargazing* (Cooper Dillon Books, 2021).

CAITLIN ROACH is a queer poet from Southern California. She holds an MFA in poetry from the Iowa Writers' Workshop and is an assistant professor-in-residence at the University of Nevada, Las Vegas. A finalist for the National Poetry Series and Tin House alum, her poems appear in *jubilat*, *Narrative*, *The Iowa Review*, *Denver Quarterly*, *Tin House*, *Colorado Review*, *Poetry Northwest*, *Poetry Daily*, and *Best New Poets 2017*, among other publications. For more, please visit caitlinroach.com.

MICAH RUELLE is queer writer, editor, and instructor residing in Minneapolis. Their chapbook, *Failure to Merge*, was published by Finishing Line Press (2019). They received their MFA in creative writing from Texas State University.

Samyak Shertok's poems appear or are forthcoming in *Blackbird*, *The Cincinnati Review*, *Gettysburg Review*, *Hayden's Ferry Review*, *The Iowa Review*, *KROnline*, *New England Review*, *Shenandoah*, *Waxwing*, and elsewhere. His work has been awarded the Robert and Adele Schiff Award for Poetry, the Tucson Festival of Books Literary Award for Poetry, and an AWP Intro Journals Award. Originally from Nepal, he is currently a PhD student in literature and creative writing at the University of Utah, where he is a Steffensen Cannon Fellow. A finalist for the National Poetry Series and the Jake Adam York Prize, he has received fellowships from Aspen Words, the Vermont Studio Center, and the Fine Arts Work Center in Provincetown.

Tyler Starks is a recent graduate of the MFA Program at Hollins University. His work appears on Poets.org. He currently lives in Brooklyn, New York.

Jessica Lynn Suchon is the author of *Scavenger*, forthcoming from YesYes Books and the winner of the Vinyl 45 Chapbook Contest. She received her MFA from Southern Illinois University where she received honors from the Academy of American Poets. Jessica has been named an Aspen Words Emerging Writer Fellow and Tennessee Playwrights Studio Fellow. Her librettos have debuted internationally in compositions by Stephanie Ann Boyd.

Jennifer Sutherland graduated from law school in 1997 and in 2020 she graduated from the Creative Writing MFA Program at Hollins University. Her work appears or is forthcoming in the *Denver Quarterly*, *I-70 Review*, *RABBIT*, *Susurrus*, and elsewhere. She lives in Baltimore.

Natalie Tombasco grew up in Staten Island, New York. She is pursuing a PhD in creative writing at Florida State University and serves as the interviews editor of the *Southeast Review*. Her work can be found in *Copper Nickel*, *Fairy Tale Review*, *Yalobusha Review*, *The Rumpus*, *Southern Indiana Review*, *Poet Lore*, *VIDA Review*, among others, and a chapbook titled *Collective Inventions* (CutBank 2021).

KATELYN BOTSFORD TUCKER is a teacher and writer in Connecticut. She received the 2019 Excellence in Teaching Award from the Connecticut Council for the Social Studies and was selected by the Gilder Lehrman Center for the Study of Slavery, Resistance, and Abolition to research apartheid in Johannesburg, South Africa. Her work has appeared in *Second Chance Lit* and *Zero Readers*.

MICHAEL VANCALBERGH currently lives in Normal, Illinois, and works at the University of Illinois Urbana–Champaign. He teaches writing, comics, and many other courses to make sure his child always has a healthy supply of cereal. His work has appeared in *Spoon River Poetry Review*, *Tinderbox Poetry*, *Apex Magazine*, *autofocus Lit*, and many other journals. His work has been nominated for a Pushcart Prize. You can find him on Twitter (@MVCpoet) or Instagram (@mvcdoesart).

DAVID JOEZ VILLAVERDE is a current MFA candidate at the Helen Zell Writers' Program at the University of Michigan. He is the winner of *Black Warrior Review*'s 2018 poetry contest. A CantoMundo Fellow, his work has appeared in *THRUSH*, *The Rumpus*, *RHINO*, and elsewhere. He can be found at schadenfreudeanslip.com

GRACE WANG is a student at Harvard College originally from Columbus, Indiana. Her work has been recognized by the National Scholastic Art and Writing Awards, *The Adroit Journal*, *Hyphen Magazine*, *The Interlochen Review*, Columbia College Chicago, and The Indiana Repertory Theatre.

JINJIN XU is a poet, artist, and filmmaker from Shanghai. Her work has been recognized by Poetry Society of America's George Bogin Memorial Award, 92Y Discovery Prize, and the Thomas J. Watson Fellowship. She holds an MFA from NYU, where she was a Lillian Vernon Fellow. Her debut, *There Is Still Singing in the Afterlife*, was selected by Aria Aber for the inaugural Own Voices Chapbook Prize; her second chapbook, *This Is My Testimony*, is forthcoming from *Black Warrior Review*. She is currently guest features director of *LIFE* China.

JAY YENCICH has published poems and reviews in venues such as *Mantis*, *Pleiades*, *Poetry Northwest*, and *The Seattle Review*. He earned his MFA from the University of Washington, where he received the Academy of American Poets Prize, and is presently a PhD candidate at the University of Illinois at Chicago, where he studies Old English, early modern British literature, and ecopoetics.

Rebecca Zweig is a poet, translator, and journalist based in Mexico City. Her work has appeared in *The Nation*, *Boston Review*, *Bennington Review*, *Hobart Pulp*, and elsewhere. She recently held a Teaching-Writing Fellowship at the Iowa Writers' Workshop.

Participating Magazines

32 Poems
32poems.com

3Elements Literary Review
3elementsreview.com

The Account
theaccountmagazine.com

The Adroit Journal
theadroitjournal.org

AGNI Magazine
agnionline.bu.edu

Alien Magazine
alienliterarymagazine.com

ANMLY
anmly.org

Appalachian Review
appalachianreview.net

Apple Valley Review
applevalleyreview.com

apt
apt.aforementionedproductions.com

Atlanta Review
atlantareview.com

Atticus Review
atticusreview.org

Barrelhouse
barrelhousemag.com

Bat City Review
batcityreview.com

Beestung
beestungmag.com

Bellevue Literary Review
blreview.org

Beloit Poetry Journal
bpj.org

Better Than Starbucks
betterthanstarbucks.org

Birdfeast
birdfeastmagazine.com

Birmingham Poetry Review
uab.edu/cas/englishpublications/birmingham-poetry-review

Blood Orange Review
bloodorangereview.com

Bloodroot
bloodrootlit.org

The Boiler Journal
theboilerjournal.com

Boulevard
boulevardmagazine.org

Boxcar Poetry Review
boxcarpoetry.com

Carve Magazine
carvezine.com

Cincinnati Review
cincinnatireview.com

Coal Hill Review
coalhillreview.com

The Rupture
therupturemag.com

Copper Nickel
copper-nickel.org

Crazyhorse
crazyhorse.cofc.edu

Cumberland River Review
crr.trevecca.edu

december
decembermag.org

Diode
diodepoetry.com

DIALOGIST
dialogist.org

Ecotone
ecotonemagazine.org

EVENT Magazine
eventmagazine.ca

Fairy Tale Review
fairytalereview.com

The Fiddlehead
thefiddlehead.ca

Fjords Review
fjordsreview.com

The Florida Review
floridareview.cah.ucf.edu

Foglifter
foglifterjournal.com

Foothill: A Journal of Poetry
cgu.edu/foothill

Free State Review
freestatereview.com

The Georgia Review
thegeorgiareview.com

The Gettysburg Review
gettysburgreview.com

Gingerbread House Literary Magazine
gingerbreadhouselitmag.com

Glass: A Journal of Poetry
glass-poetry.com/journal.html

Great River Review
greatriverreview.com

Greensboro Review
greensbororeview.org

Guernica
guernicamag.com

Gulf Coast
gulfcoastmag.org

Hamilton Arts & Letters
HALmagazine.com

Hayden's Ferry Review
haydensferryreview.com

Hominum
hominumjournal.org

Image
imagejournal.org

Iris
iris.virginia.edu

Jet Fuel Review
jetfuelreview.com

Kenyon Review
kenyonreview.org

The Lascaux Review
lascauxreview.com

Los Angeles Press
thelosangelespress.com

The MacGuffin
schoolcraft.edu/macguffin

The Margins
aaww.org

Massachusetts Review
massreview.org

Memorious: A Journal of New Verse & Fiction
memorious.org

Michigan Quarterly Review
sites.lsa.umich.edu/mqr

Minola Review
minolareview.com

The Minnesota Review
minnesotareview.dukejournals.org

Mississippi Review
www.mississippireview.com

Moonchild Magazine
moonchildmag.net

Muzzle Magazine
muzzlemagazine.com

The Nashville Review
as.vanderbilt.edu/nashvillereview

New England Review
nereview.com

Newfound
newfound.org

New Ohio Review
newohioreview.org

The Night Heron Barks
nightheronbarks.com

Nimrod International Journal
utulsa.edu/nimrod

Okay Donkey
okaydonkeymag.com

Parentheses Journal
parenthesesjournal.com

Passages North
passagesnorth.com

Permafrost
permafrostmag.uaf.edu

Pigeon Pages
pigeonpagesnyc.com

Ploughshares
pshares.org

Poem-a-Day
poets.org/poem-day

Poet Lore
poetlore.com

Poetry
poetrymagazine.org

Porter House Review
porterhousereview.org

Portland Review
portlandreview.org

Posit Journal
positjournal.com

Prism Review
sites.laverne.edu/prism-review

Psaltery & Lyre
psalteryandlyre.org

Quarterly West
quarterlywest.com

Radar Poetry
radarpoetry.com

Raleigh Review
RaleighReview.org

Rattle
rattle.com

River Styx
riverstyx.org

Roanoke Review
roanokereview.org

Room Magazine
roommagazine.com

Ruminate Magazine
ruminatemagazine.com

Salamander
salamandermag.org

The Seventh Wave
theseventhwave.co

Sewanee Review
thesewaneereview.com

Shenandoah
shenandoahliterary.org

Sine Theta Magazine
sinetheta.net

Slab
slablitmag.org

SLICE Magazine
slicemagazine.org

Slippery Elm
slipperyelm.findlay.edu

The Southeast Review
southeastreview.org

The Southern Review
thesouthernreview.org

Spillway
spillway.org

Split Lip Magazine
splitlipmagazine.com

Split Rock Review
splitrockreview.org

storySouth
storysouth.com

Sugar House Review
SugarHouseReview.com

SWWIM Every Day
swwim.org

Tahoma Literary Review
tahomaliteraryreview.com

Temporales
as.nyu.edu/content/nyu-as/as/departments/spanish/graduate/mfa/temporales.html

Terrain
terrain.org

Thrush Poetry Journal
thrushpoetryjournal.com

Tinderbox Poetry Journal
tinderboxpoetry.com

Up North Lit
upnorthlit.org

Up the Staircase Quarterly
upthestaircase.org

Virginia Quarterly Review
vqronline.org

Washington Square Review
washingtonsquarereview.com

Water~Stone Review
waterstonereview.com

Whale Road Review
whaleroadreview.com

wildness
readwildness.com

Willow Springs
willowspringsmagazine.org

The Yale Review
yalereview.yale.edu

ZYZZYVA
zyzzyva.org

Participating Programs

Binghampton University Creative Writing Program
binghamton.edu/english/creative-writing

Dominican University of California MFA in Creative Writing
dominican.edu/mfa

Florida International University MFA in Creative Writing
english.fiu.edu/creative-writing

Hollins University Jackson Center for Creative Writing
hollinsmfa.wordpress.com

Johns Hopkins The Writing Seminars
writingseminars.jhu.edu

Kansas State University MFA in Creative Writing Program
k-state.edu/english/programs/cw

McNeese State University MFA Program
mfa.mcneese.edu

Minnesota State University Mankato Creative Writing Program
english.mnsu.edu/cw

Monmouth University Creative Writing
monmouth.edu/school-of-humanities-social-sciences/ma-english.aspx

New Mexico State University MFA in Creative Writing
english.nmsu.edu/graduate-programs/mfa

New School Writing Program
newschool.edu/writing

New York University Creative Writing Program
as.nyu.edu/cwp

North Carolina State MFA in Creative Writing
english.chass.ncsu.edu/graduate/mfa

Northwestern University MA/MFA in Creative Writing
sps.northwestern.edu/program-areas/graduate/creative-writing

Ohio University Creative Writing PhD
ohio.edu/cas/english/grad/creative-writing/index.cfm

Saint Mary's College of California MFA in Creative Writing
stmarys-ca.edu/mfawrite

Sarah Lawrence College MFA in Writing
sarahlawrence.edu/writing-mfa

Southeast Missouri State University Master of Arts in English
semo.edu/english

Syracuse University MFA in Creative Writing
english.syr.edu/cw/cw-program.html

Texas Tech University Creative Writing Program
depts.ttu.edu/english/cw

UMass Amherst MFA for Poets and Writers
umass.edu/englishmfa

UMass Boston MFA Program in Creative Writing
umb.edu/academics/cla/english/grad/mfa

UNC Greensboro Creative Writing Program
mfagreensboro.org

University of Alabama at Birmingham Graduate Theme in Creative Writing
uab.edu/cas/english/graduate-program/creative-writing

University of Connecticut Creative Writing Program
creativewriting.uconn.edu

University of Idaho MFA in Creative Writing
uidaho.edu/class/english/graduate/mfa-creative-writing

University of Illinois at Chicago Program for Writers
engl.uic.edu/CW

University of Kansas Graduate Creative Writing Program
englishcw.ku.edu

University of Maryland MFA Program
english.umd.edu

University of Memphis MFA Program
memphis.edu/english/graduate/mfa/creative_writing.php

University of Mississippi MFA in Creative Writing
mfaenglish.olemiss.edu

University of New Orleans Creative Writing Workshop
uno.edu/writing

University of San Francisco MFA in Writing
usfca.edu/mfa

University of South Carolina MFA Program
artsandsciences.sc.edu/engl/mfa-program-carolina

University of Southern Mississippi Center for Writers
usm.edi/writers

University of Texas Michener Center for Writers
michener.utexas.edu

University of South Florida Creative Writing
english.usf.edu/graduate/concentrations/cw/degrees/

Vermont College of Fine Arts MFA in Writing
vcfa.edu

Western Michigan University Creative Writing Program
wmich.edu/english

West Virginia University MFA Program
creativewriting.wvu.edu

The series editor wishes to thank the many poets involved in our first round of reading:

Hodges Adams, Hajjar Baban, Betsy Blair, Kate Coleman, Henrietta Hadley, Katherine James, Wheeler Light, Madeline Miele, and Raisa Tolchinski.

Special thanks to Jason Coleman and the University of Virginia Press for editorial advice and support.